D1461654

Practice Papers for SQA Exams

General Credit

History

Text © 2009 Bruce Jamieson and Neil McLennan
Design and layout © 2009 Leckie & Leckie

01/150609

ISBN 978-1-84372-771-2

Published by
Leckie & Leckie Ltd, 3rd floor, 4 Queen Street, Edinburgh, EH2 1JE
Tel: 0131 220 6831 Fax: 0131 225 9987
enquiries@leckieandleckie.co.uk   www.leckieandleckie.co.uk

Special thanks to
A CIP Catalogue record for this book is available from the British Library.

Leckie & Leckie Ltd is a division of Huveaux plc.

Questions and answers in this book do not emanate from SQA. All of our entirely new and original Practice Papers have been written by experienced authors working directly for the publisher.

Special thanks

from Neil McLennan to Mum and Dad, as always; and to my 'history' friend Ross for his keen eye
from Bruce Jamieson to the SQA History Examination team with whom I spent many fruitful years

Introduction

Layout of the Book

This book contains exam advice and practice exam papers which mirror the actual SQA exam as much as possible. The layout, paper colour and question level are all similar to the actual exam that you will sit, so that you become familiar with what the exam paper will look like.

The answers are at the back of the book. Each answer is similar to that which would be included in the markers' guidelines. To help you discover how best to approach the various question types, this book starts off with a practical tips section. We suggest you look at this first before you attempt the practice exam papers.

Revision advice is provided in this introductory section of the book, so please read on!

How To Use This Book

The Practice Papers can be used in three main ways:

1. You can use the first section, called Exam Skills, to develop your skills on exam technique by looking at the specific types of questions and how best to answer them. The first section also allows you to see how two different students have approached each question type. By following each student and looking at their answers, you can see where they went wrong and also what they did right!

2. You can complete an entire practice paper as preparation for the final exam. If you would like to use the book in this way, you can either complete the practice paper under exam-style conditions by setting yourself a time for each paper and answering it as well as possible without using any references or notes, or you can answer the practice paper questions as a revision exercise, using your notes to produce a model answer. Your teacher may mark these for you.

3. You can use the Topic Index at the back of this book to find all the questions within the book that deal with a specific topic or a specific question type. This allows you to focus specifically on areas that you particularly want to revise or, if you are midway through your course, it lets you practise answering exam-style questions for just those topics that you have studied.

Revision Advice

Work out a revision timetable for each week's work in advance – remember to cover all of your subjects and to leave time for homework and breaks. For example:

Day	6pm–6.45pm	7pm–8pm	8.15pm–9pm	9.15pm–10pm
Monday	Homework	Homework	English Revision	Chemistry Revision
Tuesday	Maths Revision	Physics Revision	Homework	Free
Wednesday	History Revision	Modern Studies Revision	English Revision	French Revision
Thursday	Homework	Maths Revision	Chemistry Revision	Free
Friday	History Revision	French Revision	Free	Free
Saturday	Free	Free	Free	Free
Sunday	Modern Studies Revision	Maths Revision	History Revision	Homework

Make sure that you have at least one evening free a week to relax, socialise and recharge your batteries. It also gives your brain a chance to process the information that you have been feeding it all week.

Arrange your study time into one hour or 30-minute sessions, with a break between sessions e.g. 6pm–7pm, 7.15pm–7.45pm, 8pm–9pm. Try to start studying as early as possible in the evening, when your brain is still alert, and be aware that the longer you put off starting, the harder it will be to start!

Study a different subject in each session, except for the day before an exam.

Do something different during your breaks between study sessions – have a cup of tea, or listen to some music. Don't let your 15 minutes expand into 20 or 25 minutes though!

Have your class notes, and any textbooks available for your revision to hand, as well as plenty of blank paper, a pen, etc. You may like to make keyword, main people and important events sheets like the example below:

Keyword	Meaning
Propaganda	Ways in which people or organisations can persuade people (posters, radio messages, adverts).
Conscription	Being forced to join the army (introduced in Britain in 1916).
Nationalism	Having a love for your country, being patriotic.
Conscientious Objectors	People who refused to join the military because they did not believe in the war.

Finally, forget or ignore all or some of the advice in this section if you are happy with your present way of studying. Everyone revises differently, so find a way that works for you!

Transfer Your Knowledge

As well as using your class notes and textbooks to revise, these practice papers will also be a useful revision tool as they will help you to get used to answering exam-style questions. You may find as you work through the questions that they refer to a topic that you haven't come across before. Don't worry! You should be able to transfer your knowledge and skills to a new example. The section at the front of this book will demonstrate how to answer all the various question types you will get asked in a Standard Grade History exam. The technique for answering the various questions is the same, no matter what topic area it is asking about.

Learning Styles

We all have different learning styles and we would suggest you look at your learning style before you begin to use this book. Ask your teacher for help in this area before you start. If you work best on your own, then go for it! If you work best with a partner, you could ask your partner to help mark your work using this book. Research shows that one of the best ways to learn is by teaching other people. With this in mind, you should read about a question type or topic and then think of ways in which you could teach other people.

Modern Revision Aids

As mentioned above, there are many ways to revise. Not all of these involve simply using paper and pen. Modern technology can be used to help you when revising for exams. Mobile phones and MP3 players can be used to record your revision notes. Camcorders, cameras or mobile phones can be used to capture images of mind maps and spider diagrams that you and your friends have made. You could use this book to make up mind maps on the various topics that might come up in the Standard Grade History exam. Or you could make up mind maps of the question types and how to answer them. The key point is; there are lots of ways to revise and some of them can be quite fun.

Command Words

In the practice papers and in the exam itself, a number of command words will be used in the questions. These command words are used to show you how you should answer a question and some words indicate that you should write more than others. If you familiarise yourself with these command words, it will help you to structure your answers more effectively.

More advice is given on how to identify types of question using command words and then how to answer them, in the Exam Skills section of this book.

Command Words	Meaning/Explanation
Describe	Give a detailed account of an event or reason for something happening.
Explain	Discuss why an action has been taken or why something happened; what are the reasons and/or processes behind it? Make sure you have enough detail and have *fully* explained what is being asked.
How Important	Discuss the reason mentioned in the question, but also write about other reasons that are important but not mentioned in the question.
Compare	Give the key difference or similarities between two sources.
Assess	Weigh up factors/consider various options.
How Fully	To what extent does a source explain or describe an action or an event.

In the Exam

Before the exam be clear exactly what you are going to do. The practice papers will help you to become familiar with the exam's instructions. Remember that in the real exam there is a choice of Contexts in each unit. Make sure that you know the three Contexts you have been studying and that you are going to tackle in the exam.

Read the question thoroughly before you begin to answer it – make sure you know exactly what the question is asking you to do. For longer answers, like the Credit 8 mark essay, you could perhaps plan your answer by jotting down a few keywords, a mind map or a reminder of the important things to include in your answer. You could cross them off as you deal with them and check them before you move on to the next question, to make sure that you haven't forgotten anything. However, be careful about how much time you have got. Do not run out of time. Here is a summary of your possible time allowance. You can always adapt it to your own way of working.

GENERAL LEVEL	CREDIT LEVEL
• You have 90 minutes to answer questions on three topics (Unit Contexts).	• You have 105 minutes to answer questions on three topics (Unit Contexts).
• There are 20 marks allocated for KU questions and 30 marks for ES questions.	• There are 24 marks allocated for KU questions and 36 marks for ES questions.
• Allow a few minutes to read each question thoroughly.	• Allow a few minutes to read each question thoroughly.
• Make sure you know exactly what the question is asking you to DO.	• Make sure you know exactly what the question is asking you to DO.
• Allow about 15 minutes in total for thinking and planning – about 1 minute per question.	• Allow about 20 minutes in total for thinking and planning (including time to organise your 8 mark essay response).
• You have about one and a half minutes **per mark** to write your answer to each question.	• You have just under one and a half minutes **per mark** to write your answer to each question.
• A 4 mark question should be answered in about 6 minutes.	• A 5 mark question should be answered in about 7 minutes.

OTHER USEFUL ADVICE

Don't repeat yourself, as you will not get any more marks for saying the same thing twice.

Give proper explanations. A common error is to give descriptions rather than explanations. If you are asked to explain something, you should be giving reasons. Check your answer to an 'explain' question and make sure that you have used plenty of linking words and phrases such as 'because', 'this means that', 'therefore', 'so', 'so that', 'due to', 'since' and 'the reason is'. Do not leave the marker thinking 'so what' at the end of any sentence you have written.

In KU at General Level, **use the sources provided**. Some questions will ask you to 'describe' or 'explain' and provide a source for you to work from. Make sure that you take any relevant information from these sources and then add in your own knowledge. By adding both information from the source and information from your own knowledge you will have a fuller and better answer.

Always **do something with the evidence presented** – do not just copy it out. Try to write answers in your own words.

At both KU and ES always try to **bring in your own knowledge** – the information you have learned and remembered from your history course at school.

Good luck!

Topic Index

Topic/Paper	Gen Paper 1	Gen Paper 2	Gen Paper 3	Credit Paper 1	Credit Paper 2	Credit Paper 3
Unit 1B: Changing Life in Scotland and Britain 1830 – 1930						
Population	KU Q2		All ES	KU Q1	KU Q1	All ES
Agriculture			KU Q2			
Health and Housing			KU Q1		All ES	
Coal Mining	KU Q1	All ES		KU Q2		KU Q1
Women & the Vote		KU Q1		All ES		
Railways	All ES	KU Q2			KU Q2	
Unit 2A: International Conflict and Co-operation						
Causes of World War I	KU Q1	All ES		KU Q1		KU Q1
Recruitment	ES Q3, ES Q4	KU Q1				
Trench Warfare	KU Q1 ES Q5		KU Q1	All ES	KU Q1	ES Q3
The Home Front			All ES		All ES	
German Home Front / German Defeat		KU Q2	KU Q2			
Treaty of Versailles						ES Q4 & 5
League of Nations						KU Q2
Unit 3D: People and Power – Germany 1918 – 1939						
The Weimar Republic		KU Q1	KU Q1	KU Q1	KU Q1	KU Q1
Economic problems- Ruhr Crisis and Inflation	KU Q1					
Hitler's Step to Power 1929–1933	KU Q2		All ES	All ES		
Hitler becomes dictator 1933–1934	All ES			KU Q2	KU Q2	
Life in Nazi Germany	All ES	KU Q2	KU Q2	All ES	All ES	KU Q2 All ES

(continued)

Topic/Paper (Continued)	Gen Paper 1	Gen Paper 2	Gen Paper 3	Credit Paper 1	Credit Paper 2	Credit Paper 3
KU Question Types						
Describe (KU1)	Unit 1Q1 Unit 1 Q2	Unit 1 Q1 Unit 3 Q2	Unit 1 Q1 Unit 2 Q2 Unit 3 Q2	Unit 3 Q1	Unit 1 Q1	Unit 2 Q1 Unit 2 Q2 Unit 3 Q2
Explain (KU2)	Unit 1 Q2 Unit 3 Q1	Unit 1 Q2 Unit 2 Q2 Unit 3 Q1	Unit 1 Q2	Unit 1 Q1 Unit 3 Q2	Unit 1 Q2 Unit 2 Q2	Unit 3 Q1
How important (KU3)	Unit 2 Q1 Unit 3 Q2	Unit 2 Q1	Unit 2 Q1 Unit 3 Q1	Unit 1 Q2 Unit 2 Q1 *	Unit 2 Q1 # Unit 3 Q1	Unit 1 Q1 ~
8 mark essay (Credit Papers only)	NA	NA	NA	Unit 1 Q1 *	Unit 2 Q1 #	Unit 1 Q1 ~
ES Question Types						
How useful (All units) (ES1)	Unit 1ES Q3 Unit 2 Q3	Unit 1ES Q3 Unit 2 Q4	Unit 1ES Q3 Unit 2 Q3	Unit 1ES Q3 Unit 3 Q3	Unit 1ES Q3 Unit 2 Q2	Unit 1ES Q3 Unit 3 Q3
Select and organise evidence (Unit I only) (ES5)	Unit 1ES Q4	Unit 1ES Q4	Unit 1ES Q4	Unit 1ES Q4	Unit 1ES Q4	Unit 1ES Q5
Reach a conclusion (Unit I only) (ES6)	Unit 1 ES Q5	Unit 1 ES Q5	Unit 1 ES Q5	Unit 1 ES Q5	Unit 1 ES Q5	Unit 1 ES Q5
Compare sources (Unit II & III only) (ES2)	Unit 2 Q4 Unit 3 Q4	Unit 2 Q5 Unit 3 Q4	Unit 2 Q4 Unit 3 Q4	Unit 2 Q3 Unit 3 Q4	Unit 3 Q4	Unit 2 Q5
Assess the attitude (Unit II & III only) (ES3)	Unit 2 Q5	Unit 3 Q3	Unit 3 Q5	Unit 2 Q2	Unit 2 Q3 Unit 3 Q3	Unit 2 Q4
Assess the completeness of a source(s) (ES 4) (Unit II&III only)	Unit 2 Q3	Unit 2 Q3	Unit 3 Q3	Unit 2 Q4	Unit 2 Q3	Unit 2 Q3 Unit 3 Q4

Exam Skills

SECTION ONE: EXAM SKILLS

PART ONE: KNOWLEDGE AND UNDERSTANDING

There are three types of Knowledge and Understanding question. All of them can appear in any unit, and in either General or Credit papers:

- Type 1 (KU1) is a 'Describe' question.
- Type 2 (KU2) is an 'Explain' question.
- Type 3 (KU3) is a 'How Important' question.

Always look at the number of marks allocated and remember the rule:
One relevant point = one sentence = one mark.

Type 1 (KU1) 'Describe' Questions

These questions are designed to test your knowledge and understanding of an event or the results of an event. The questions should be relatively straightforward as long as you have done some revision before trying the question. The question usually starts with the words 'Describe...' or 'What...'. For example, 'Describe the sort of jobs done by Irish immigrants in Scotland in the late 19th and early 20th centuries.' Or, 'What were the results of the 1923 economic crisis for the German people?' At General Level you will be provided with a source to help you answer the question. You should aim to include two or three pieces of information from the source. Be careful with this! Not all the information in the source will help you answer the question. Some information may be a 'distracter' and not relevant to the question. Be sure only to write out information which directly answers the question. Once you have used the source you will need to add in information from your own knowledge to help you get full marks. If you only use the source, you cannot get full marks. Likewise, if you only use your own knowledge you risk not getting a good mark.

At General Level, attempt to use the source and add further information from your own knowledge. Use the number of marks available as a guide as to how many points you should include in your answer. Make sure you write in full sentences and not in bullet points.

At Credit Level you will not get any source. You will be provided with a short 'trigger sentence', which is there to get you thinking about what's coming up in the question. All the points must come from your own knowledge in a Credit KU question. The points must be well developed, with good detail and in separate sentences. Roughly aim for one sentence per mark and do not write in bullet points, as this will not get you good marks.

Here is a typical, General Level 'Describe' question. Remember to use the source to get some points, then add in further information from your own knowledge.

Read **Source A** and try to answer the question which follows it.

Source A is from, 'Germany 1918–1939' by John Kerr.

Source A

In 1923, the Nazis attempted to seize power in Munich and overthrow the Bavarian Government. With the collapse of this Beer Hall Putsch, most people believed that Hitler and the Nazis were finished. But the trial gave Hitler much needed national publicity. He was photographed standing beside General Ludendorff, which made people think Hitler was an important person. When he was found guilty, Hitler was given a short prison sentence.

---

1. Describe the results of the 1923 Beer Hall Putsch. **3 marks**

The question is out of 3 marks – so you need three pieces of information describing what happened as a result of the Beer Hall Putsch. You should make points that are included in the source and you must also add one or two points from your own knowledge.

Look at the first example of a student's answer. This answer was by **Tom**:

1. *'Hitler had tried to take over the Bavarian Government but it failed. Hitler got his photo with General Ludendorff which made people think he was important. Hitler was sent to jail after the attempted take over.'*

✓ Imagine you are the marker!

A marker will look at this answer and give marks for two areas: information which comes from the source (Presented Evidence or **PEv**) and also the candidate's own information (recalled information or **R**). After each tick, the marker will put either **PEv** or **R** depending on which category this falls into. Before we look at how Tom actually got on, have a try marking his answer for yourself. How many marks do you think Tom should get?

This would score 2 out of 3 marks at General Level. Tom has clearly given three pieces of information and has set them out in three developed sentences. However, all the information has come from the source and he has not added anything from his own knowledge. Therefore Tom cannot be awarded full marks for his answer.

Now look at **Amy**'s answer:

1. *'In 1923 Hitler had tried to take over the government in Bavaria with the Beer Hall Putsch. Many of Hitler's followers were injured or even killed by police marksmen. Hitler failed, but it was not all bad. Hitler got some good national publicity and had his photo taken with General Ludendorff, who was a World War I hero. Hitler was sent to jail but even this was a good thing for Hitler. He used the court case to get even more publicity. He also wrote his book "Mein Kampf" when in prison.'*

This scores full marks – 3 out of 3 (3/3). Amy has used the source but has also added in information from her own knowledge. Look at the source again and then look at her answer. See if you can find which bits she has taken from the source and which bits she has added in from her own knowledge.

Remember, at General Level, if you only use material from the source you cannot get full marks for KU questions. You must use your own knowledge.

Now we will look at a Credit example:

Remember, at Credit Level there is no source, just a 'trigger sentence'. This will not actually help you answer the question and you will need to use recall throughout your answer.

By the summer of 1914, Europe was on the brink of a world war. The war would lead to the death of a whole generation of men.

---

2. Describe the alliance system in Europe before the First World War. **4 marks**

Tom has been revising a lot for Unit II (International Conflict and Cooperation). Here is his answer to a KU1 'Describe' question in a Credit paper. How did he do this time?

Tom's answer:

2. 'Before World War One, Europe was split into two armed camps. But they were very different from each other. The Triple Alliance had Germany, Austria-Hungary and Italy in it. They had joined together and agreed to help each other in a war. The Triple Entente were not all committed to joining each other in a war as it was only an entente. The Triple Entente started off with France and Britain joining together. Soon Russia joined and the Triple Entente was set up.'

✓ <u>Imagine you are the marker!</u>

Remember, in the previous section we said that a marker will look at this answer and give marks for two areas: information which comes from the source (Presented Evidence or **PEv**), and also the candidate's own information (recalled information or **R**). **However**, in Credit the candidate can only use their own information as there is no source. The marker would simply use ticks and the letter **R** when marking a credit answer. Now, you try to mark Tom's credit answer. Does he have enough points to get full marks?

Tom has given a strong answer and has clearly been revising. He has clearly developed points and has answered the question well. Tom scores 4/4.

Amy was not as strong in her Credit answer:

2. There were alliances in Europe before the war. On one side the Entente had Russia, France and Britain. On the other side was Germany, Austria-Hungary and Italy in the Triple Alliance.

Amy has not done as well with this answer. Her first sentence does not really answer the question and then she only follows it up with two very limited point of recall. Amy scores 2/4.

Type 2 (KU2) 'Explain' Questions

The second kind of KU skill asks you to explain an event or issue. Once again, these should be straightforward as long as you have revised three units for the exam. Good revision will boost your confidence and ensure you are able to write strong, developed answers in the final exam. In an 'explain question' you are being asked to explain an action, an event, or the results of an event. These questions usually start with the words 'Explain...' or 'Why...'. For example, 'Explain why many people benefited from the coming of the railways.' Or, 'Why did so many Scottish people move to large towns in the nineteenth century?'

At General Level the source will contain points to help you answer the question. Aim to use some of the reasons but also include your own recalled information.

At Credit Level you will not be provided with a source. Before the question, there will be a short 'trigger sentence'. This will not help you greatly in your attempt to answer the question. At Credit you will need to use recalled information only.

To get a good mark at Credit Level you must make sure the recalled information is fully developed. Your answer should be clear and quite detailed. Make sure each sentence answers the question directly. Do not waffle and go off the question.

In both General and Credit Levels you should look to see how many marks the question is worth. This will give you an idea of how many developed sentences you should have in your answer. You must write in full sentences. Bullet pointed answers will not get you good marks and should be avoided.

One additional hint:

Make sure you do actually explain what the question is asking. Many candidates do not fully explain what they are trying to say and do not link their answers directly to the question. This can leave the marker thinking 'so what?' at the end of each sentence you have written. Some candidates assume that the marker knows what is in the candidate's mind. **Do not assume anything!** Write everything out clearly and fully for the marker. After all, the exam is an opportunity for you to show off what you have learned!

Here is a sample Credit 'Explain' question:

The population of Scotland went up throughout the nineteenth and early twentieth centuries.

---

1. Explain why the population of Scotland went up from 1830 to 1930. **4 marks**

Amy's answer:

1. 'The population of Scotland went up very quickly from 1830 to 1930. New houses were built to replace the slums. The railways helped to bring fresh food to the towns. Hospitals and doctors also now had new medicines.'

✓ <u>Imagine you are the marker!</u>

Again, the only code a marker will use in this answer is an **R**. Look at Amy's answer and put ticks where you would give her a mark. Has she properly *explained* why the population of Scotland went up from 1830 to 1930?

You can tell by the length of the answer that Amy is not going to get 4 marks. Her first sentence does not answer the question directly. Sentence two is a factor in population rise but she does not fully explain how this led to the population going up. If she had said something like the following sentence, she would have properly explained her answer: *'New houses replaced the slums, which meant better living conditions and fewer deaths.'*

Tom's answer:

1. The population went up for three main reasons. There were fewer deaths because of better medical knowledge and more medicines being available. There was also better housing, so fewer people died of diseases such as cholera and TB. The birth rate also went up at certain points, such as the baby boom. Also there were lots of new people coming to Scotland and Britain from other countries, causing our population to go up.

Tom scores 4/4: Not only does he include four points but he also makes sure these points fully explain why the population went up.

Type 3 (KU3) 'How Important' Questions

In the third type of Knowledge and Understanding question, you must assess the importance of one 'factor' (reason or cause) in an event, or the cause of an event. You should mention whatever 'factor' is given in the actual question itself. However, this **may** not be enough for an answer in this type of question. Whatever topic the question is about will have a number of factors that caused it. This is especially important in Credit Level, where you will need to know all the factors as there will be no source to prompt you in your answer.

Try this example:

The event which finally triggered war came on 26 June 1914 in Sarajevo, a town in the Austro-Hungarian province of Bosnia.

1. How important were the assassinations of the Archduke Franz Ferdinand and his wife in causing the First World War? **4 marks**

Amy's answer:

1. 'In 1914 the Archduke of Austria-Hungary and his wife Sophie were in Bosnia. They were shot by a man called Gavrilo Princip, who was in the Black Hand Gang. Princip shot Franz Ferdinand whilst he was in his car. He did not die immediately, but some time afterwards. Princip was quickly arrested and sent to jail. World War One caused millions of deaths when soldiers died on the Western Front because of Franz Ferdinand's death.'

✓ Imagine you are the marker!

Again, we are looking at a Credit example here and the only code for a marker to use is **R**. When you read Amy's answer, think – has she actually said how important the assassinations were in causing the war? Has she identified any other factors that may also have caused the war?

Amy has not really understood the question. Although she has written quite a lot, her response does not answer the question. The task she was being asked to complete is a '**How Important**' question. Instead, Amy has **described** the assassinations. She probably scores 1 mark for the point in the last sentence. She does not mention any other factors that caused World War One so she cannot score any more marks. Amy scores 1/4.

Look at **Tom's** answer:

1. The assassination of Franz Ferdinand caused World War One because Austria blamed Serbia for shooting their heir to the throne. Austria-Hungary gave Serbia an ultimatum which they had to agree to in 2 days. When Serbia did not agree this led to war. But there were other things that caused the war. The naval arms race meant that Britain and Germany had lots of Dreadnoughts and countries had weapons ready to fight with. Alliances also caused the war, as a small event could cause lots of countries to join the war. Also, empires caused the war, as countries like Germany wanted to have an empire like Britain's and got very jealous.

Tom has produced a good answer. He talks about how important the assassinations were in causing the war. He then goes on to mention three other factors (arms race, alliances and rivalries over empires). Tom scores 4/4.

The 8 Mark Question

This type of question appears only in the Credit paper.

This can be any of the previously shown types of Knowledge and Understanding question, but it is often a 'How Important' question or sometimes an 'Explain' question that is used for an 8 mark essay. There are some basic rules you need to stick to when answering the 8 mark question.

It is very important that you structure your answer. You must include an introduction, paragraphs and a conclusion. Have you heard your teacher saying an essay is like a hamburger? It needs a start (roll), middle pieces (the meat and bits of salad) and an end (roll).

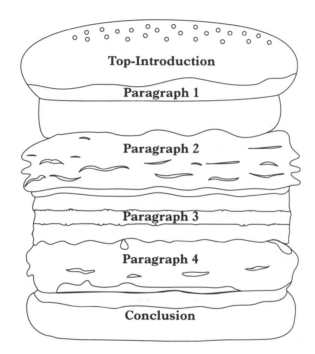

Other teachers refer to an essay being like a dinosaur, with a head, body and tail. Whatever the example, it is vital the essay has an introduction, middle part and a conclusion. Without this structure you cannot get full marks. The structure itself is worth 2 marks.

Before you start writing your answer for the 8 mark question, it is important that you organise your thoughts. Take a moment to think carefully about what information you are going to include in your answer and that it is presented in an organised manner. Be clear about what you are going to write in this extended piece of writing before you put pen to paper. Remember you can write on the exam paper and you may want to underline what the key topic of the question is. You may also want to scribble a couple of key points down to refer to as you start to write the 8 mark answer.

Start with an introduction. This does not need to be too long. Your introduction should make clear the main points you will develop in the following paragraphs.

The middle section should include separate points which are relevant to the question. They should be fully developed and explained. You should write the middle part of the essay in separate paragraphs.

Your conclusion should sum up all the things you have just talked about and it must directly answer the question. If it is a 'How Important' question, you will be talking about lots of different reasons for something happening. You may want to end by simply saying that there are lots of reasons for events happening and then pick the most important reason that your 8 mark essay has identified.

Do not spend too long on the extended essay question. However, it is worth 8 marks, which is roughly double the marks you get for other questions in the exam. The amount of time you spend on the 8 marker should reflect this. Aim to spend about 10–12 minutes in total writing for this question. You may take a couple of minutes to plan and write your introduction at the start. So in total a maximum of 12–14 minutes is recommended.

Look through the sample papers at the back of this book and pick out the 8 mark questions. Have a go at answering them. You can then try to self-mark them or get a friend or your teacher to look over your answer. Have you included an introduction, a middle part and a conclusion? Have you written in paragraphs? Does your middle part have enough points of information? Is it all relevant to the question and explained properly? Have you scored 8 marks out of 8?

Good luck in the KU section. As this section has taught you, the key to success is plenty of revision and lots of practice of the various types of question. Once you are confident with KU you should move on to the next section and learn about Enquiry Skills (ES) questions and how to answer them.

PART TWO: ENQUIRY SKILLS

There are six types of Enquiry Skills question. Type 1 questions can appear in any unit, Type 5 and Type 6 questions only appear in Unit I. The others can appear in Unit II or Unit III – or in both units. All appear in General and Credit papers.

- Type 1 questions (ES1) ask you 'How Useful' something is.
- Type 2 questions (ES2) ask you to 'Compare Sources'.
- Type 3 questions (ES3) ask you to 'Assess an Attitude'.
- Type 4 questions (ES4) ask you to 'Assess the Completeness of a Source or Sources'.
- Type 5 questions (ES5) ask you to 'Select and Organise Evidence'.
- Type 6 questions (ES6) ask you to 'Reach a Conclusion'.

Remember:

1. Look at the number of marks allocated and remember the rule:

    One relevant point = **one sentence** = **one mark**

2. **Always answer the question**

    If the question asks whether a source is useful, actually write your opinion by saying, 'Source A is useful because...' or 'Source A is quite useful because...', and then go on to explain why. If the question asks you to show agreement between sources, make sure that in your answer you say something like, 'The two sources agree to quite an extent about...'. If the question asks you to explain how fully a source describes or explains something, always answer that question by saying 'Source A describes... to an extent...'.

    At General Level, you actually get a mark for doing this – i.e. for showing the correct process in ES1, ES2, ES4 and ES6 items.

Type 1 (ES1) 'How Useful' Questions

These questions are designed to test your ability to evaluate a source; to say why it is useful to a historian. This is an important skill, as it determines whether a piece of evidence has any historical value or whether it is flawed, incomplete, exaggerated or not backed up by other evidence. You should always be accurate in your response to the question. Make very definite statements – **and always answer the question**. State clearly whether, in your opinion, the source is useful or of limited use.

Here is a typical source and an evaluation (How Useful) question. Remember that the introductory information before the actual source is very helpful, especially in this type of question.

Read **Source A** and try to answer the question which follows it.

Source A was said by the Rev. Donald McColl, giving evidence to the 1883 Royal Commission of Inquiry into the South Uist Clearances.

Source A

> I remember those dreadful days back in 1851. I saw many being forcibly evicted from their crofts. They were bound hand and foot, and packed off like cattle on board the vessel to Canada. Although later some crofters chose to emigrate to join family, the recollections of ill-treatment towards many, in those earlier days, operates unfavourably on the minds of the present generation towards emigration.

1. How useful is **Source A** as evidence of the Highland Clearances in the mid-nineteenth century?   **4 marks**

This is a Credit Level question and is out of 4 marks – so you need four pieces of evidence to argue that the source is useful – or limited in its use. The points you make can be about the **authorship** of the source (whether reliable or not); the **date** it was written; the **purpose** of the source, the **content** of the source, the **accuracy** of the source (always backed up by additional, recalled evidence) and perhaps the **limitation**; what it does not tell you.

This answer was written by **Tom**:

1. 'Source A was written by the Rev. Donald McColl. It was written at the time. It tells you lots of stuff about the Clearances and I know it's all true.'

> ✓ <u>Imagine you are the marker!</u>
>
> A marker will look at this answer and give marks for seven areas: (1) Does it answer the question? If so, the marker would put **P**, to show that the process was complete. (This would merit a mark at General Level but not at Credit.) The marker would then look for evidence to show that Tom has backed up his judgement through the use of (2) authorship (putting an **A** if so); (3) date (**D**); (4) purpose (**Pu**); (5) content (**C**); (6) accuracy (**Ac**); or (7) limitation (**L**). Finally, the marker would make sure that Tom has given four pieces of evidence in order to get full marks. How many marks do you think Tom should get?

Tom's answer would score 0 marks at Credit Level. It does not answer the question: is the source useful? It is not precise in its information. Why is the Rev. McColl a reliable person? Can we believe him? Did he actually witness the events for himself? What exact piece of information in the source helps us to research the Highland Clearances? Are you convinced that Tom actually knows that the described events are accurately recorded? Does he answer the question at all?

Now look at **Amy's** answer:

1. 'This is a useful source as it was written by a reliable person – an eyewitness of a clearance. It is a primary source written later than the events it describes but from first-hand knowledge of a mid 19th-century eviction. It tells us useful information such as that crofters were forced to leave their land. It backs up my own knowledge of the time when Highlanders were burned out of their houses and forced to emigrate.'

This scores 4 marks: 1 for accurate authorship (**A**); 1 for detailed time period (**D**); 1 for selected, useful content (**C**) and 1 for accuracy (**Ac**) – reinforced by correct, recalled knowledge. It also makes a judgement about the source and thus completes the required process (**P**) by saying 'This is a useful source.'

Amy could also have said that the source is believable, as it was written for a precise, historical purpose – to give information to a Royal Commission – a major government enquiry. It would also have been possible to say that the author was perhaps biased or was exaggerating, as he had been directly affected by the events he describes. It could also be said that he was interviewed many years after the events and that his memory may have been affected by the passage of time.

There is no 'right' answer. There are many ways of answering this question. You just have to apply any four pieces of relevant, precise information. If it is a primary source – that is, one written at (or close to) the time of the issue/event being discussed, then always make precise authorship and time statements. **Do not just repeat a rehearsed set of phrases:** a formula or a mantra. Do not allow the examiner to say 'so what?' or 'where?' in response to anything you write, for example, 'It was written by a man' (so what?) 'who was there' (where?) 'at the time' (what time?). Always be detailed and exact.

If you do have a formula, eg: **ABCD** = **A**uthorship; **B**ias; **C**ontent; **D**ate, then make sure you adapt it to suit the source and the question.

At General Level, it is permissible to say that a source is useful as 'it is a primary source written at the time (of the investigation)' but this will not get a mark at Credit Level, where the 'time statement' must be more precise, eg: 'at the time of the Highland Clearances in the mid-nineteenth century'.

Do not simply write that a source is useful because, 'it is written by a doctor'; 'it comes from a newspaper'; 'it was said by a minister'; 'it comes from the lips of a politician'; 'it was written by Hitler'. You must explain why that makes the source of value as evidence, eg, 'It is written by a doctor who would be aware of the medical problems in the mid-nineteenth century'; 'It is an editorial from a reputable newspaper, outlining the opinion of the editor'; 'It is written by a reliable witness who has no reason to lie'; 'It was written by Adolf Hitler – the leader of the German Nazi Party'.

Be detailed, be accurate, be relevant: be a historian! Remember – actually answer the question! No 'How Useful' (ES1) item ever asks you to simply say if a source is useful. The question will always ask you to evaluate the source for a given reason. You are to assess its usefulness for a specific purpose. Always direct your answer to that purpose.

Remember: if all you mention is the content of the source (what it says), you will only score 1 mark in total.

The same rules apply if you are asked to evaluate a secondary source: evidence which was written after an event.

How would you assess **Source B** for usefulness? It was written by History professor Hew Strachan in his book, *The First World War*, published in 2006.

Source B

> Throughout the war, rats did more than just disturb the soldiers' sleep; they carried disease and they spoilt food. Trench warfare provided ideal conditions for their multiplication. They thrived on its debris, including the bodies of the unburied dead.

2. How useful is **Source B** as evidence of conditions in the trenches during World War One?   **4 marks**

Tom has been practising this skill. Here is his second answer to a 'How Useful' (ES1) Credit Level question. How did he do this time?

Tom's answer:

2. *'Source B is quite useful as it tells us about the rats being a nuisance in the trenches. It doesn't mention lice but I know they were also a problem. However, the source was written in 2006 by a man who wasn't even in the trenches so what does he know about life then? He is a professor so he could be very absent-minded.'*

✓ Imagine you are the marker!

Remember the marker's rules: does Tom answer the question? If he does, write the letter **P.** Does he correctly show useful authorship (**A**), date (**D**), purpose (**Pu**), content (**C**), accuracy (**Ac**) or limitation (**L**)? Try to mark Tom's Credit answer. How many correct points of evidence does he give? How many marks out of 4 does he get this time?

Tom starts off well. He selects good content to illustrate the value of the source as evidence of trench conditions. He then accurately establishes what the source does not tell us and brings in good recalled evidence to prove it. However, he then makes the mistake of saying that a secondary source is not as useful as a primary source as it does not actually date from the time of the event. He should have realised that the author of a 'history book' will have researched the period thoroughly and given a balanced account, based on the discovered and assessed evidence. The author will also have the benefit of hindsight, being able to look back on events with an open mind.

Remember: good secondary sources are as useful as primary sources.

Tom only scores 2/4. (He would have scored 3/4 at General Level – why is this?)*

Amy's answer was better:

2. *'Source B is really useful as it informs us that rats were indeed a great problem in the trenches of World War One. The author is a history professor who will have researched a lot of facts about the period. He is not actually involved but then will not be so wrapped up in the problem – he is able to look back and come to an impartial judgement. However, this is just one piece of evidence. There were many other problems in the trenches such as the horrible, deep mud.'*

Amy scores 4/4: 1 mark for well selected content; 1 mark for a good point about authorship; 1 mark for recognising that the author is writing from a position of hindsight and 1 mark for limitation of content.

Type 2 (ES2) 'Compare Sources' Questions

The second kind of Enquiry Skill asks you to compare sources. This is a useful thing to do as evidence from a second source can either reinforce a previous piece of information or it can counter it. **A developed comparison is best** – and is rewarded with 2 marks.

A developed comparison is where you first make a simple, general point of comparison, linking the two sources, and then develop that statement by quoting from each source, eg, 'The two sources agree that... as Source A says... and Source B agrees by saying...'

This is true at both General and Credit levels.

*At General Level, Tom would have obtained a 'process point' for saying that the source is useful and correctly reinforcing that judgement.

Try this example:

Look at **Source C** and then answer the question, comparing it with what is said in **Source A**, which is printed again below.

Source C was written by a modern historian.

Source C

When harvests failed, especially in the mid-nineteenth century, many people in the Highlands and Islands had no option but to turn to their landlord. Sometimes he helped them. At other times, he thought them ignorant and lazy and treated them badly. Many were cruelly evicted from their crofts and forced to go elsewhere. Thousands chose voluntarily to emigrate to Canada. Others resisted and had to be persuaded. The issue is still debated today by many who continue to feel very angry about the Clearances.

Source A

I remember those dreadful days back in 1851. I saw many being forcibly evicted from their crofts. They were bound hand and foot, and packed off like cattle on board the vessel to Canada. Although later some crofters chose to emigrate to join family, the recollections of ill-treatment towards many, in those earlier days, operate unfavourably on the minds of the present generation towards emigration.

3. To what extent do **Sources A** and **C** agree about emigration from Scotland in the mid-nineteenth century?   **5 marks**

Amy's answer:

3. The sources agree a lot about emigration from Scotland as they both talk about emigration and say that it happened a lot. Source A says 'towards emigration' and Source B says 'to emigrate'.

✓ Imagine you are the marker!

A marker would read Amy's answer and write **SC** next to each simple comparison and award 1 mark. The marker would then look to see if Amy had developed that comparison and, if so, would write **DC** for a developed comparison and award it another mark. How many marks do you think Amy got for her answer?

You can tell by the length of her answer that Amy is not going to get 4 marks. She does not make any real connection between the sources. She makes a very general and unhelpful comment about emigration. She does not select accurate quotes to reinforce her argument. A kind marker might award 1 mark to Amy for saying that both sources agree that emigration from Scotland did occur frequently in the mid 19th century! Many markers would give her no marks at all.

You must always do something with the evidence. It is not good practice to simply copy out what one source says – and then what the other source says. You must demonstrate a historical skill and show that you really understand what the sources are about and how they agree or disagree.

Tom's answer:

3. The two sources agree that many Scots emigrated in the mid 19th century as Source A says 'I saw <u>many</u> evicted and packed on board a vessel to Nova Scotia' and Source C agrees by saying that <u>thousands</u> chose to emigrate. The sources also agree that many Scots went to Canada. The sources also agree that some people did emigrate because they wanted to. Source A says that later people went to join their family and Source C says thousands chose to emigrate.

✓ Imagine you are the marker!

Now, try to mark Tom's answer, remembering to write **SC** for a simple comparison, worth 1 mark, and **DC** for a developed comparison, worth 2 marks. At General Level, would he get an extra mark for showing the correct process?*

Tom scored 5/5 with two developed points of comparison about the scale of emigration and the reasons for emigration, and one simple point of comparison about where Scots emigrated to.

Tom could also have said, 'The Sources agree that many Scots emigrated as they were forced off their land. Source A mentions ill treatment of the evictions and Source C says many were cruelly evicted and forced to go elsewhere.'

It would also have been possible to say that both sources agree that cruel methods were used to persuade people to emigrate. Can you find the key passages in each source to expand this statement into a developed comparison worth 2 marks?

In some questions, you may be asked to identify points of disagreement. In either case, it is quite permissible to bring in points of agreement and disagreement. The question will always ask 'how far' or 'to what extent' sources agree or disagree.

---

*Tom does not need it, but at General Level he would score an additional mark for saying, 'The two sources agree...' and then backing up that statement with correct information.

Type 3 (ES3) 'Assess an Attitude' Questions

The third type of Enquiry Skill is to determine or discuss the attitude of the author of a source. Once again, you must answer the question. What is the author's point of view or opinion or emotional response? What does the author really feel about something or some issue? You should use emotive words to describe how the author feels. Is he or she angry, pleased, opposed, biased, horrified, supportive etc? Always state the obvious by writing something along the lines of, 'This author does not like'; 'the writer is violently against...'; 'the cartoonist is obviously showing his displeasure at...' etc.

You can then back up your chosen comment with relevant quotes from the passage, drawing attention to the particular expression you have used. At Credit Level, the question usually asks you to 'discuss' the attitude of an author. This is so that you can bring in any recalled knowledge you have about the author, or the sentiment expressed. At General Level, you will more often be asked to identify and/or describe the attitude(s) expressed in the source.

Try this example:

4. Discuss the attitude of the author of **Source D** towards conditions in the trenches during the First World War. **4 marks**

Source D was written by Lieutenant Burke, a soldier in World War One.

Source D

> When we got told the attack was cancelled, we were disappointed. We just wanted to leave the trench. The conditions in it were miserable. You lived cave-like. You can imagine a man after being in one of those mud-holes for a week, where he couldn't properly wash. I hated it. The men were hardened but even so! A further problem was trench fever. It left you weak and listless.

Amy's answer:

4.   I don't think that Mr Burke was very happy. He says we were disappointed and you lived cave like. He also says you can imagine a man being there. It is a very useful source.

> ✓ Imagine you are the marker!
>
> A marker would try to determine whether Amy had answered the question, and then check if she had properly described what the author's feelings were, with selected quotes from the source to illustrate those feelings and reinforce her statement. Try to mark Amy's answer, putting a tick at each correctly identified and reinforced point of view.

Amy has not really understood the question. It is not asking her to evaluate the source for usefulness. It is asking her to discuss the feelings of the author: what does he think about trench conditions? **She probably scores 1 mark** for a general (holistic) statement about the author's overall opinion but that is all. Her other evidence does not back up her initial comment.

Now look at **Tom's** answer:

4.   Lt. Burke hates the trenches. He complains that they were like living in a cave, which means they were wet and uncomfortable. He particularly dislikes being dirty – saying he hates not being able to wash. He loathes the conditions, calling them 'miserable'. He admits that you got used to it but even so his opinion is that it was really horrible, with diseases like trench fever that made you very ill.

Tom has written a good answer, with some recall. He uses helpful 'buzz' words like 'hates', 'complains', 'dislikes', 'loathes' and 'horrible', and reinforces these with accurate, selected extracts from the source. Tom scores full marks (4/4).

Type 4 (ES4) 'Assess the Completeness of a Source or Sources' Questions

The fourth kind of Enquiry Skill tests your ability to select evidence from a given source and use it, along with recalled evidence, to address a given issue. This type of question usually begins 'How fully does ...' or 'To what extent does ...'. It is important to remember that you **must use the source** and establish what evidence it provides towards answering the question and then **provide additional evidence from your own recalled knowledge**. You cannot score full marks if you fail to do either of these things.

Look at **Source E** and attempt the question which follows it.

Source E was written by Professor Gerhard Rempel in *The Nazi Road to Power*.

Source E

> In January 30, 1933, Hindenburg received Hitler in audience and appointed him chancellor. This was a great hour for the Nazis. Hitler had not seized power. He had come to office by a sordid, backstairs intrigue and with the president's consent. He was chancellor, but in a government of 'national concentration'. There were in fact only two Nazis in the cabinet. Papen, vice-chancellor in the new cabinet, was pleased by the success of his intrigue, believing that he had taken Hitler prisoner. 'In two months we'll have pushed Hitler into a corner so hard that he'll be squeaking', Papen boasted to a friend.

5. How fully does **Source E** explain why the Nazis came to power in 1933?
    You must use evidence **from the source** and **your own knowledge** and give
    reasons for your answer.   **5 marks**

Amy's answer:

5. Source E explains a little about the immediate coming to power of the Nazis. It reveals that Hitler was appointed chancellor as the result of political bargaining. His opponents thought that they would be able to use and control him. The source does not go into the background reasons for the Nazi success. It does not mention their growing support from many who hated the Weimar government. It does not point out the Nazi appeal due to their attack on the Treaty of Versailles. It does not go into the fact that Hitler himself was becoming more and more popular due to his public speaking at huge rallies.

✓ Imagine you are the marker!

Once again, as a marker, you need to be sure that Amy has actually done what she has been asked to do. Does she assess the completeness of Source E – and show what's missing? You should mark Amy's answer by putting an **S** in the margin next to any relevant piece of evidence she has selected from the source *and* the letter **R** next to any item of recalled information she brings in. Amy can only score full marks if there is at least one **S** and one **R** in the margin. How many points of evidence does she give? What does she score?

Amy answers the question well. She actually says that the source is helpful but incomplete, so the process is up front. She does not go into all the reasons why the Nazi party seized power but she doesn't need to. She uses two pieces of evidence from the source and gives three relevant pieces of recalled evidence, giving her full marks: 5/5.

Tom meanwhile, makes mistakes. Can you spot them in his answer, given below?

Tom's answer:

5. Hitler came to power because many people voted for him. He was very popular because he attacked the Communists. He was a good speaker and made people listen to him.

Tom cannot get full marks as he does not use the source at all. His three points of evidence are all from recall. In addition, he does not answer the question. He does not state an opinion as to the completeness of the source. Thus, he loses a process mark, giving him only 2/5.

Type 5 (ES5) 'Select and Organise Evidence'and Type 6 (ES6) 'Reach a Conclusion' Questions

The final two types of Enquiry Skill, 'Select and Organise Evidence' (ES5) and 'Reach a Conclusion' (ES6) appear together in Unit I only. They always come after a 'How Useful' (ES1) question, which has already asked you to establish the usefulness of one source for a given purpose – 'the issue for investigation'.

The investigation takes the form of a statement with which you are asked to agree, disagree or partly agree. The issue might be:

- 'The Suffragettes lost support for the votes for women campaign.'
- 'The worst problem facing Scottish cities in the 19th century was poor housing.'
- 'The railways were welcomed by everyone in Scotland.'

Let's use **Sources A** and **C** again to help us address a General Level issue:

The issue for investigation is:

People in the Highlands and Islands of Scotland were always driven away by force from their land.

It has already been established that **Source A** is useful for investigating the Highland Clearances and emigration from Scotland.

The next question (ES5) asks you to select evidence from **Source A** and one other source at General Level; with two other sources at Credit Level. You are allowed **in this response only** to write bullet points and/or to present your evidence in the form of a table – if you so choose. (Remember that you will be penalised in every other response if you do not write in proper sentences.)

Source A was said by the Rev. Donald McColl, giving evidence to the 1883 Royal Commission of Inquiry into the South Uist Clearances.

Source A

> I remember those dreadful days back in 1851. I saw many being forcibly evicted from their crofts. They were bound hand and foot, and packed off like cattle on board the vessel to Canada. Although later some crofters chose to emigrate to join family, the recollections of ill-treatment towards many, in those earlier days, operate unfavourably on the minds of the present generation towards emigration.

Source C was written by a modern historian.

Source C

> When harvests failed, especially in the mid-nineteenth century, many people in the Highlands and Islands had no option but to turn to their landlord. Sometimes he helped them. At other times, he thought them ignorant and lazy and treated them badly. Many were cruelly evicted from their crofts and forced to go elsewhere. Thousands chose voluntarily to emigrate to Canada. Others resisted and had to be persuaded. The issue is still debated today by many who continue to feel very angry about the Clearances.

6. What evidence in **Source A** agrees with the view that people in the Highlands and Islands were driven by force from their land?

   What evidence in **Source C** disagrees with the view that people were driven by force from their land?   **5 marks**

   Here is **Tom's** answer, which he chose to give as a chart.

6.	*Source A: for the issue*	*Source C: against the issue*
	saw many being forcibly evicted	harvests failed and they had to go
	people were bound hand and foot	people had no option but to turn to landlords for help
	people were packed off like cattle	thousands chose voluntarily to go

✓ Imagine you are the marker!

As a marker you need to ask yourself three questions: (1) does Tom select evidence for and against the issue? (He must have at least one piece of evidence on both sides.) (2) Does Tom clearly lay out his selected evidence? (3) Does he have at least five pieces of correct evidence in total? Mark Tom's answer and if you say 'yes' to each question, you can give him full marks: 5/5.

Tom has laid his selected evidence out well. He has chosen six good pieces of evidence – just to be sure, although only five relevant pieces are required. He has selected good quotes from the sources and has not made them too short. He has not used ellipses – where you just give the first few words and then add dots, eg: 'saw many being…'

Amy chose a slightly different approach.

Amy's answer:

6. It says in Source A that they were dreadful times and that many were forcibly evicted. It says that many were tied up and packed off in a ship to Canada. It says that there was a lot of ill treatment. In Source C it says that people had to leave when they had no food left. It also says that people were desperate and had to ask their landlord to help them. It also says that they chose to go by themselves.

This is a good answer at General Level – although it takes much longer to construct than Tom's chart. It is also not quite so easy to see both sides of the argument and it might be penalised at Credit Level for not making this clear.

A chart for the ES5 (Select and Organise Evidence) question might make it easier to complete the last Enquiry exercise (ES6) – using the collected evidence **and your own recalled evidence** to address the issue given at the start of the investigation.

7. How far do you agree that people in the Highlands and Islands of Scotland were always driven away by force from their land?   **4 marks**

Amy's answer:

7. There were dreadful times and many were forcibly evicted. Many were tied up and packed off in a ship to Canada. In Source C it says that people had to leave when they had no food left. It also says that people were desperate and had to ask their landlord to help them. It also says that they chose to go by themselves.

Amy just repeats the evidence she collected for question 6. She doesn't do very much with it. Nor does she always make it clear that she is using presented evidence. More importantly, she does not bring in any recalled evidence and so does not use her own relevant, remembered information. By simply using evidence from the presented evidence (**Sources A** and **C**), she cannot score full marks. In addition, she doesn't answer the question and doesn't make a judgement on how far people were driven by force out of the Highlands. Consequently, she does not gain a process mark. So 3 pieces of presented evidence = only 3 marks in total.

Not bringing in any recall at Credit Level is even more serious. There are 5 marks for this question at Credit Level, and without demonstrating recall you cannot score pass marks, you can only achieve a maximum of 2/5 marks.

Tom's answer:

7.   As it says in Source A, many people were driven out of the Highlands during the Clearances. Their homes were burned down so they had nowhere to go. Many had to emigrate to England or abroad. However, as the modern historian rightly says, many Scots chose to emigrate – either to find work or to join relatives. I know myself that many Scots did well overseas and helped to make modern Canada. So not all Scots had to leave – but many were driven away.

> ✓ <u>Imagine you are the marker!</u>
>
> Having looked at Amy's mistakes, try to mark Tom's response. Remember to ensure that: (1) he has used evidence from the source; (2) he has brought in recalled knowledge; (3) he has shown balance in his answer – i.e. given both sides of the argument; (4) he has made a judgement – i.e. answered the question; (5) he has given at least four pieces of evidence. If you say 'yes' to each of these five points, you can award four marks.

Tom uses two points from the sources – one from each side of his chart – ensuring a balanced answer. He makes it clear that he is using the presented evidence by saying 'as it says in Source A'. He then brings in three points of recall: that people had their homes burned and had to leave; that people went overseas to find work; that many Scots became very active in Canadian life. He even directs the marker to the fact that he is using recalled evidence by saying 'I know myself'. He reaches a fair judgement in his last sentence. If he had needed it, Tom would have gained a process mark for arriving at and stating this conclusion. However, he already has a clear 4 out of 4 possible marks.

It is even more important at Credit Level to achieve balance in the conclusion. Both sides of the argument must be shown – and a clear judgement reached. If this is not done you will lose a 'process mark'. The Credit 'Reach a Conclusion' (ES6) question is out of 5 marks.

USING ILLUSTRATED SOURCES

Sources using photographs, paintings, cartoons, posters, charts or other illustrated material can be used in an examination. The skills required to tackle Enquiry questions about them are just the same as those needed for textual sources – bearing in mind the fact that you are not dealing with words alone.

Look at the cartoon shown in **Source A** and try to answer the set of questions which follow. The correct answers are given like the answers to a real SQA examination. These are called 'Marking Instructions' and use bullet points to guide the marker. Remember that you must not use this way of writing answers yourself, except in your reply to a 'Select and Organise Evidence' (ES5) item. In **every other response** you must always answer in proper sentences.

Source A was drawn by British cartoonist David Low on 3 July 1934, three days after the Night of the Long Knives. It shows Adolf Hitler with the gun, Hermann Goering beside him with a spear and Joseph Goebbels under his legs.

Source A

They salute with both hands now.

There are several possible ways to answer illustrated sources questions. The answers are given here as bullet points so that you can see quickly and easily the full range of possible answers you could include. Don't forget though – bullet point answers in the exam are not acceptable: when you're taking the exam, you must always put your answer into full sentences!

8. How useful is **Source A** as evidence of reaction to the Night of the Long Knives?   **4 marks**

Answer:

8. A good answer will include a balanced evaluation of **Source A** using evidence such as:

   - Authorship: British cartoonist concerned about the events in Nazi Germany
   - Date: Primary source written at the time of the Night of the Long Knives
   - Content: Shows Germans/the German army were frightened of Hitler
   - Accuracy: Agrees with the fact that Hitler shot members of the German army/got rid of opposition to his rule
   - Purpose: To make people realise how serious things were under Hitler
   - Limitation: Only one British man's view/not everyone agreed that Hitler was dangerous   **ES1 (4 marks)**

Remember, you only need four of the above points for 4 marks.

Look carefully at how many marks are allocated for the rest of the questions.

9. What is the attitude of the author of **Source A** towards Adolf Hitler? **3 marks**

   Answer:

9. Evidence from the source about the attitude of David Low towards Hitler is:

   - **Does not like** him
   - **Hates** his bullying ways
   - **Worried** that he is getting too powerful
   - **Concerned** that he is killing people   **ES3 (3 marks)**

10. To what extent does **Source A** show what happened on the Night of the Long Knives?   **4 marks**

    Answer:

10. To answer this question well you should assess the completeness of **Source A,** using **presented evidence** such as:

    - Shows Hitler/the Nazis killed people
    - Shows the Nazi leaders (Hitler, Goering, Goebbels) were in charge
    - Shows Hitler was prepared to kill anyone who was in his way
    - Shows Germans who once saluted Hitler with one arm now raise both in surrender

and **recall** such as:

    - Operation Hummingbird was designed to get rid of powerful SA leaders
    - Many people died during the purge (numbers vary from 85–400)
    - Important officials such as Ernst Roehm were killed

- Other political opponents were shot
- Von Schleicher, Gregor Strasser and von Kahr were murdered
- Hitler tried to hush up the events   **ES4 (4 marks)**

Look at **Source A** again and compare it with **Source B**.

Source B is from the Spartacus History website.

> By 1934, Hitler constantly feared that he might be overthrown by others who
> wanted his power. Along with his henchmen, Goering and Goebbels, he planned
> action. In late June 1934 Hitler, gun in hand, personally arrested the SA leader,
> Ernst Roehm. During the next 24 hours, 200 other SA officers were arrested.
> Many were shot as soon as they were captured. Hitler explained why he did it.
> 'In this hour I become the supreme judge of the German people. I gave the
> order to shoot the ringleaders of a plot against me.' Hitler had made it clear that
> he was the supreme ruler of Germany.

11. To what extent do **Sources A** and **B** agree about Hitler's role in the Night of the
    Long Knives?   **5 marks**

    Answer:

11. A high scoring answer will assess agreement between the sources using evidence
    such as:

    - *Sources agree that the Night of the Long Knives was planned by Hitler,**
      Goering and Goebbels:

Source A says/shows:	Hermann Goering, Joseph Goebbels and Hitler threatening others
Source B says:	Along with his henchmen, Goering and Goebbels, Hitler planned action

    - *Sources agree that Hitler was involved in the events:**

Source A shows:	Hitler with a smoking gun
Source B says:	Hitler arrested Roehm, gun in hand

    - *Sources agree that Hitler gave the order to shoot people:**

Source A shows:	Hitler in charge/the most aggressive figure
Source B says:	(Hitler) gave the order to shoot the ringleaders

    - *Sources agree that Hitler was the unquestioned leader:**

Source A shows:	Hitler in charge/everyone obeying Hitler
Source B says:	He was the supreme ruler of Germany

    One mark for a simple comparison (*)

    Two marks for a developed comparison.   **ES2 (5 marks)**

Exam A – General Level

History   Standard Grade: General

Practice Papers   **Exam A**
For SQA Exams   **General Level**

You are allowed 1 hour and 30 minutes to complete this exam.

Answer all questions from all three Units.

Choose only **one** Context from each Unit, then answer the questions in **both** Section A **and** Section B (Knowledge & Understanding **and** Enquiry Skills). **Please note this book only contains Contexts Unit IB, Unit IIA and Unit IIID as these are the most popular units in Scottish Schools.**

The complete list of Contexts in this exam is shown below:

      Unit I – Changing Life in Scotland and Britain
          Context B: 1830s–1930s   **Pages 40–41**

      Unit II – International Conflict and Cooperation
          Context A: 1890s–1920s   **Pages 42–44**

      Unit III – People and Power
          Context D: Germany 1918–1939   **Pages 45–46**

Use information from the sources and your own studies in your answers.

Some sources have been changed to meet the needs of this exam.

Scotland's leading educational publishers

UNIT I – CHANGING LIFE IN SCOTLAND AND BRITAIN

CONTEXT B 1830s–1930s

SECTION A: KNOWLEDGE AND UNDERSTANDING

Study the information in the sources. You must also use your own information in your answers.

Source A is from a history textbook written by Wendy Doran and Richard Dargie.

Source A

> At the start of the nineteenth century all the jobs in the coal mine were done by hand. Families worked together cutting, gathering and carrying coal to the surface. After 1850 new methods and machines were developed to speed up production. At first, ponies were used to drag coal wagons to the surface. Later, steam engines did this, as well as winding the men up and down in safety cages. Railways carried the cut coal to the market.

1. Describe some of the new technology used in Scottish coal mines by 1930.   **3**

Source B is from the *Dictionary of Scottish History*.

Source B

> Scotland's population is recorded by the Registrar General for Scotland at new Registrar House, Edinburgh. The Registrar General organises a census taken every ten years to monitor the size of the population. Census results show that better medical care produced a slow decline in the death rate from the 1870s, but mortality nevertheless remained higher in Scotland than in England. Medical improvements contributed to falling mortality through the provision of infirmaries. Improved living standards also reduced the number of deaths in Scotland.

2. Explain why the population of Scotland went up between 1830 and 1930.   **4**

SECTION B: ENQUIRY SKILLS

The issue for investigating is:

> Railway development between 1830 and 1930 was always welcomed in Scotland.

Study the sources carefully and answer the questions which follow.
You should use your own knowledge where appropriate.

Source C is from *Hansard*, a record of Parliamentary debates for August 1895.

Source C

> The Chancellor of the Exchequer said that he was in favour of awarding a grant for the building of a West Highland railway. It would be for the benefit of a poor and neglected district of Great Britain. It would not only be of great advantage to the crofters and farmers of the district, but would also promote greatly the fishing interests of the people of the Western Highlands.

3. How useful is **Source C** for investigating railway development in Scotland in the nineteenth century?

3

Source D is from *Railway Records* in the National Archives of Scotland.

Source D

> Railway construction dramatically altered the landscape of 19th and early 20th century Scotland. Photographs and drawings exist to show the huge impact of the construction of the Forth Railway Bridge in the 1880s. There are also photographs and records relating to the Tay Bridge. This was the longest rail bridge over water in Europe but unfortunately it collapsed in 1879, killing 75 passengers.

4. What evidence is there in **Source C** that the railways were welcome in Scotland?

   What evidence is there in **Source D** that the railways were **not** welcome in Scotland?

5

5. To what extent do you think that railway development between 1830 and 1930 was always welcomed in Scotland?

4

You must use evidence **from the sources** and **your own knowledge** to come to a conclusion.

[End of Context IB]

Marks

UNIT II – INTERNATIONAL CONFLICT AND COOPERATION

CONTEXT A 1890s–1920s

SECTION A: KNOWLEDGE AND UNDERSTANDING

Study the information in the sources. You must also use your own information in your answers.

Source A is from a school history textbook on World War One.

Source A

> Although most of the people who lived in these newly independent countries (in the Balkans) were Slavs, they competed with each other from the start. This rivalry was often based on mistrust and hatred that went back hundreds of years. As a result, independence for these countries did not end the problems of this area; it only led to more tension between the nations.

1. How important was nationalist feelings in the Balkans in causing World War One? **3**

Source B is from letters written by Norman Collins in October 1916, from the Western Front.

Source B

> Yesterday I had tea with the Brigadier General as he was so pleased with the work we have done. His dugout was a splendid place, not like ours. The mud is really awful. Even on the main roads it is up to our boot tops and off the road will drag a man's boots off with puttees on. In the trenches it varies from ankle to almost waist deep and men have to be hauled out sometimes with ropes. The weather is beastly and we are at present in an open field.

2. What difficulties did soldiers face in the trenches in World War One? **4**

SECTION B: ENQUIRY SKILLS

The following sources are about the experiences of soldiers during World War One.

Study the sources carefully and answer the questions which follow.
You should use your own knowledge where appropriate.

Source C is a British recruiting poster of 1914.

Source C

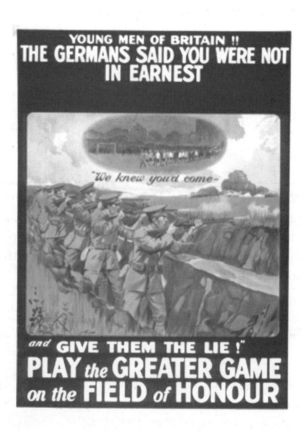

3.   How fully does **Source C** describe the reasons why young men joined the British
     army in 1914?   **3**

You must use evidence **from the source** and **from your own knowledge** and
give reasons for your answer.

Marks

Source D was said by Willie Macmillan who fought in World War One.

Source D

> We thought it was our duty to go. It would be great fun – a great game. We would beat the Germans and come back with the trophy – get a hero's welcome. And we all wanted the uniform – it would impress the lassies in the High Street. I played a lot of football and I was annoyed when the Germans said that we were all cissies – that we were not brave enough to come and fight. We showed them – but at a terrible cost.

4.   How far do **Sources C** and **D** agree about why young men volunteered to fight in World War One?   4

Source E is written by Captain L. Spicer in July 1916.

Source E

> I am feeling thoroughly cheerful: happier than I've felt for many months past. In the first place, I believe and hope that the battle is being a success, a great success. At first I was very depressed at our losses. So many people gone who I miss so much! But, I have the consolation that these brave men gave their lives for a successful effort and not in a forlorn hope.

5.   What did the author of **Source E** think about fighting in World War One?   3

[End of Context IIA]

UNIT III – PEOPLE AND POWER

CONTEXT D: GERMANY 1918–1939

SECTION A: KNOWLEDGE AND UNDERSTANDING

Study the information in the sources. You must also use your own information in your answers.

Source A is from *The Weimar Republic* by Ruth Henig.

Source A

> At the height of the Ruhr crisis, the German state was in considerable danger of collapse. Extremist groups were not slow to exploit the crisis for their own advantage. Communists in Saxony and in Thuringia were working to lay the basis for a more socialist government. There was a communist rising in Hamburg. On the great East Elbian estates, Free Corps volunteers waited expectantly for a call to arms against the French.

1. In what ways did the Ruhr crisis in 1923 cause the collapse of the Weimar Government in Germany?

    3

Source B is from *The Coming of the Third Reich* by Richard J. Evans. (2003).

Source B

> Social and cultural factors accounted for the Nazis' appeal, rather than economic ones; for the unemployed voted Communist, not Nazi. Workers who were still in jobs in September 1930 were fearful of the future. They frequently turned to the Nazis to defend themselves against the looming threat of the Communist Party. The Nazis made speeches promising to cut unemployment.

2. How important was Hitler's promise of creating jobs in him gaining popularity amongst the German people?

    4

SECTION B: ENQUIRY SKILLS

The following sources are about the Nazis in power.

Study the sources carefully and answer the questions which follow.
You should use your own knowledge where appropriate.

Source C is from the German newspaper *Dachauer Tageblatt* for 6th April 1933.

Source C

> Police Commissioner of Munich, Heinrich Himmler, has announced that the first concentration camp will be opened on Wednesday near Dachau. All Communist criminals who threaten the security of the state will be arrested by the police forces and assembled here. Leaving Communists in the courthouse jails is not possible for the long term. On the other hand, it is not appropriate to let them go free again. The camp will reassure the national population. Herr Himmler further said that such protective custody would not go on any longer than necessary.

3. How useful is **Source C** as evidence of Nazi methods of control in the 1930s?   4

Source D is from www.historylearningsite.com

Source D

> Communist opponents of the Nazis, arrested by the police or the Gestapo, were sent to the nearest police cell. Those in custody were told to sign an 'Order for Protective Custody'. By signing this, they agreed to go to prison. Those who did not sign it were beaten until they did. Once an order was signed, you were sent to a concentration camp. How long you stayed there depended on the authorities. You had to prove that you had 'learned your lesson' and would behave in an acceptable manner once outside of prison. This rarely happened.

4. To what extent do **Sources C** and **D** agree about the treatment of communist opponents of the Nazis?   4

[End of Context IIID]

[End of question paper]

Exam B – General Level

History — Standard Grade: General

Practice Papers
For SQA Exams

Exam B
General Level

You are allowed 1 hour and 30 minutes to complete this exam.

Answer all questions from all three Units.

Choose only **one** Context from each Unit, then answer the questions in **both** Section A **and** Section B (Knowledge & Understanding **and** Enquiry Skills). **Please note this book only contains Contexts Unit IB, Unit IIA and Unit IIID as these are the most popular units in Scottish Schools.**

The complete list of Contexts in this exam is shown below:

Use information from the sources and your own studies in your answers.

Some sources have been changed to meet the needs of this exam.

Scotland's leading educational publishers

Marks

UNIT I – CHANGING LIFE IN SCOTLAND AND BRITAIN

> ### CONTEXT B 1830s–1930s

SECTION A: KNOWLEDGE AND UNDERSTANDING

Study the information in the sources. You must also use your own information in your answers.

Source A is from *The Story of Britain* by Roy Strong.

Source A

> By the end of the nineteenth century, the suffrage movement was already underway and in 1897 the National Union of Women's Suffrage Societies was formed. Women's magazines and sections in newspapers also reflected women's desire for changes and to be recognised. Increasingly, intelligent women could shift for themselves and would organise speeches.

1. Describe some methods used by the Suffragists in trying to get votes for women.

3

Source B is from a book about the coming of the railways by A.F. Garnett.

Source B

> Whatever the name, the function of public transport remains the same: carrying large numbers of urban and suburban people to work or to school. Or it can be for visits or entertainment and then bringing them back home again. So successful were the railways that some towns later built underground rail systems. By the 1840s, Britain was experiencing 'Railway Mania'.

2. Explain why the railways brought benefits to people living in Scottish towns.

4

SECTION B: ENQUIRY SKILLS

The issue for investigating is:

The working life of a Scottish coalminer was better than that of other workers in the nineteenth century.

Study the sources carefully and answer the questions which follow.
You should use your own knowledge where appropriate.

Source C is from a report by Robert Franks on the 'Employment of Young Persons in the Collieries of the East of Scotland' in 1842.

Source C

[Margaret Hipps]

I watched Margaret Hipps at work. Nowhere else do people work like this. It is incredible to believe that human beings can do such work, crawling on hands and knees down the mine. Dragging the tub full of coal is even more difficult because of the slope in many pits in the East of Scotland. She never leaves the dark interior, eating a bit of bread down below.

3. How useful is **Source C** for investigating conditions in the coal mines of Scotland in the nineteenth century?

3

Source D is from *Working Colliers* by G. Williams.

Source D

Part of the pride which the collier had in his position in society came from the fact that his job was one which required great strength. Colliers were proud of their work and the great skill they had to show in doing it. Down below, they were their own bosses. Compared to workers in the cotton mill, they were more independent. No one told them what to do. They were usually paid for the amount of work they did. As coal was needed more and more, so their wages went up, as long as they kept fit, and there was coal in their seam.

4. What evidence in **Source C** shows us that the life of a worker in a Scottish coal mine was very hard?

    What evidence in **Source D** shows us that the life of a coal miner was not so bad? **5**

5. How far do you agree that the working life of a Scottish coal miner in the nineteenth century was better than that of other workers in the nineteenth century? **4**

You must use evidence **from the sources** and **your own knowledge** to come to a conclusion.

[End of Context IB]

UNIT II – INTERNATIONAL CONFLICT AND COOPERATION

CONTEXT A 1890s–1920s

SECTION A: KNOWLEDGE AND UNDERSTANDING

Study the information in the sources. You must also use your own information in your answers.

Source A is an account from Robert Irvine who joined Kitchener's army in 1914.

Source A

> I was only a shop assistant at the time, and on reflection I think I volunteered because I wanted to escape from the humdrum life behind a grocer's counter. I have since been sorry that I took the decision. I was just swept up by the wave of patriotism that swept the county. When Lord Kitchener's pointing finger was on every hoarding throughout the country on a poster saying, 'Your King and Country Needs You', I was one of the innocents who were caught up in this web of patriotism.

1. How important was propaganda in encouraging men to join the army in World War One?   **3**

Source B is about the situation in Germany by 1918 (from a historian writing in 1963).

Source B

> Germany had not imported much food before the war. By 1916 the Germans had already started the story that their food shortage was due to the British 'hunger blockade'. The truth is that the Germans starved themselves. They took millions of working men away from the land for the armies. High prices encouraged peasants to send their pigs and cattle to the market. Then supplies ran short.

2. Explain why German civilians were experiencing difficulties by 1918?   **4**

Marks

SECTION B: ENQUIRY SKILLS

The following sources are about the coming of the First World War.

**Study the sources carefully and answer the questions which follow.
You should use your own knowledge where appropriate.**

Source C is a chart showing some important dates in the Naval Race between
Britain and Germany.

Source C

1906	Launching of HMS *Dreadnought* at Portsmouth
1907	'Rheinland' ships (similar to 'Dreadnoughts') built in Germany
1908	German Navy Law amended (4 'Rheinlands' now to be built instead of 3)
1909	Britain orders 8 'Dreadnoughts' instead of 3
1912	Germany competes by announcing an increase in ships
1914	Britain has 29 'Dreadnoughts'; Germany has 17

3. How fully does **Source C** show the naval rivalry which existed between Britain
    and Germany before World War One?

    4

Source D from the Constitution of the Black Hand Organisation, 1911.

Source D

Unification or Death

The organisation is an absolutely secret one. It is established
for the purpose of realising the national ideals – the Unification
of all Serbs in an enlarged state of Serbia. It will carry out a
revolutionary organisation in all the territories where Serbians
are living. It will fight with all means against all enemies of
this idea.

4. How useful is **Source D** as evidence of the problems in the Balkans before World
    War One?

    3

Source E is from www.spartacus.schoolnet.co.uk

Source E

In May 1911, ten men in Serbia formed the Black Hand Secret Society. The main
objective of the Black Hand was the creation, by means of violence, of a Greater
Serbia. Its stated aim was to create a powerful Serbian nation. It set out to use
terrorist action, as shown in its seal with its death head symbol.

5. To what extent do **Sources D** and **E** agree about the Black Hand?

    4

[End of Context IIA]

UNIT III – PEOPLE AND POWER

CONTEXT D: GERMANY 1918–1939

SECTION A: KNOWLEDGE AND UNDERSTANDING

Study the information in the sources. You must also use your own information in your answers.

Source A is from Richard J. Evans, *The Coming of the Third Reich* written in 2003.

Source A

> The most dramatic and serious effects of the financial collapse were on the price of food. A women sitting down in a café might order a cup of coffee for 5,000 marks and be asked to give the waiter 8,000 for it when she got up to pay an hour later. A kilo of rye bread, that staple of the German daily diet, cost 163 marks on 3rd January 1923, more than ten times that amount in July, and 9 million marks on 1st October 1923.

1. Explain why German people faced difficulties during the hyperinflation crisis.   **3**

Source B is (about the Nazi treatment of Jewish people).

Source B

> The Jews of Germany had been among Europe's most assimilated, most cultured, most active contributors to the national life of the state in which they lived. Then came the Nazi boycott of Jewish shops. During these boycotts Stormtroopers painted the Star of David on the windows of Jewish owned shops. "They meant to dishonour us" one Jew said at the time. Other shops had placards stuck to their windows and the daubing of their window panes.

2. Describe the methods used by Hitler to make German Jews feel inferior.   **4**

Marks

SECTION B: ENQUIRY SKILLS

The following sources are about attitudes towards the Nazis coming to power.

Study the sources carefully and answer the questions which follow.
You should use your own knowledge where appropriate.

Source C is a cartoon from the British magazine *Punch*, published on 8th March 1933.

Source C

3. What was the attitude of the author of **Source C** towards the election in Germany in March 1933?

3

Source D is from www.wikipedia.org

Source D

A German election was held on March 5 1933, and was the last to be held in Germany before World War Two. It was hardly a fair and democratic election. It took place shortly after the Reichstag fire, in which the German parliament was set alight. This event gave Hitler more power to take strong action to ensure the result went his way. To further assure that the outcome of the vote would be a Nazi win, Nazis controlled the voting process, often using bullying methods.

4. To what extent do **Sources C** and **D** agree about the March 5th election in Germany in 1933?

4

[End of Context IIID]

[End of question paper]

Exam C – General Level

History   Standard Grade: General

Practice Papers   **Exam C**
For SQA Exams   **General Level**

You are allowed 1 hour and 30 minutes to complete this exam.

Answer all questions from all three Units.

Choose only **one** Context from each Unit, then answer the questions in **both** Section A **and** Section B (Knowledge & Understanding **and** Enquiry Skills). **Please note this book only contains Contexts Unit IB, Unit IIA and Unit IIID as these are the most popular units in Scottish Schools.**

The complete list of Contexts in this exam is shown below:

        Unit I – Changing Life in Scotland and Britain
            Context B: 1830s–1930s   **Pages 60–61**

        Unit II – International Conflict and Cooperation
            Context A: 1890s–1920s   **Pages 62–63**

        Unit III – People and Power
            Context D: Germany 1918–1939   **Pages 64–65**

Use information from the sources and your own studies in your answers.

Some sources have been changed to meet the needs of this exam.

Scotland's leading educational publishers

UNIT I – CHANGING LIFE IN SCOTLAND AND BRITAIN

CONTEXT B 1830s–1930s

SECTION A: KNOWLEDGE AND UNDERSTANDING

Study the information in the sources. You must also use your own information in your answers.

Source A is a picture drawn by J.O. Brown of the collapse of a tenement in Edinburgh High Street on 24 November 1861.

Source A

1. Describe housing conditions in Scottish towns in the nineteenth century.   3

Source B is from a school textbook written by Larry Cheyne and Sandra Chalmers.

Source B

Bell's reaper, introduced widely in 1850, meant that one man, with two horses, could do the work of a dozen men. But the changes did mean unemployment. Even the growth industries and the improvements in roads and railways had a downside. Agriculture was no different. A steam threshing machine could, in a day, prepare as much grain, all threshed, cleaned, and ready for sale, as a dozen men, using flails, would in a month!

2. Why had working conditions improved for some farm workers by 1930?   4

Marks

SECTION B: ENQUIRY SKILLS

The issue for investigating is: Scotland's population grew between 1850 and 1914 due to improvements in the provision of food.

Study the sources carefully and answer the questions which follow. You should use your own knowledge where appropriate.

Source C is from *The Scottish Nation* by History professor, T.M. Devine.

Source C

> An important factor in population growth was a decline in the death rate of children. From a mid-nineteenth century peak of 130 children in every 1000 dying before reaching the age of one, the rate fell to 109 in 1914. A crucial factor in this was the health of mothers. Many women were becoming better nourished and their well-fed babies lived. Cheaper food prices helped. So too did the import of more foodstuff from overseas. Hygiene conditions also improved in the towns.

3. How useful is **Source C** for investigating the causes of population growth in Scotland between 1850 and 1914?

3

Source D is from *The Oxford Companion to Scottish History*.

Source D

> Population change results from the difference between number of births and number of deaths. It is also affected by immigration and emigration. From the early 1870s, the national death rate in Scotland went down. It was especially reduced in the cities as living standards improved. Environmental conditions involving the health of the people slowly improved. In addition, the people in the urban areas could more easily get plenty of food from the surrounding countryside.

4. What evidence in **Source C** agrees with the view that improvements in the provision of food caused the population of Scotland to grow?

   What evidence in **Source D** suggests that other factors in Scotland were causing the population to grow?

5

5. How far do you agree that Scotland's population grew between 1850 and 1914 due to improvements in the provision of food?

4

   You must use evidence **from the sources** and **your own knowledge** to come to a conclusion.

[End of Context IB]

Marks

UNIT II – INTERNATIONAL CONFLICT AND COOPERATION

> ### CONTEXT A 1890s–1920s

SECTION A: KNOWLEDGE AND UNDERSTANDING

Study the information in the sources. You must also use your own information in your answers.

Source A is from the memoirs of Robert M. Greig, a soldier on the Western Front.

Source A

> When we came up the line, the artillery fire was very intense. Both sides were hammering away at each other with great enthusiasm. I may mention that on this front the artillerymen of both sides had ample gunfire practice and were quite accurate. All hours of the day and night were made hideous with the continual thunder of all calibres of artillery. I was terrified of the shriek of the passing shells, and the thuds of their detonation.

1. How important was artillery as a weapon in World War One?   **3**

Source B is a map showing Germany's western frontier after the Versailles Treaty.

Source B

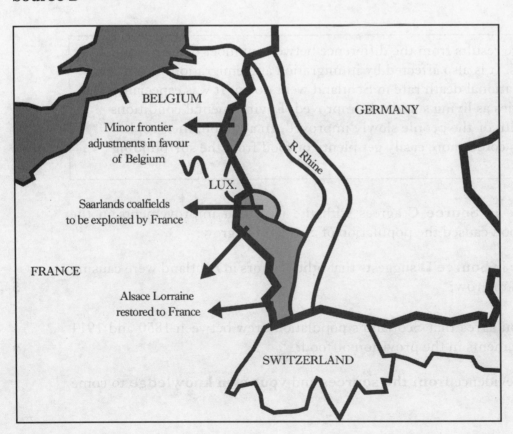

2. Describe the land terms imposed on Germany in the Treaty of Versailles?   **4**

Marks

SECTION B: ENQUIRY SKILLS

The following sources are about are about German civilians during World War One.

Study the sources carefully and answer the questions which follow.

You should use your own knowledge where appropriate.

Source C is a photograph taken in Berlin in early1918. It shows German women having to exchange potato peelings for firewood.

3. How useful is **Source C** as evidence of conditions in Germany towards the end of World War One?

3

Source D is a description of life in Germany in 1918.

Source D

> The longer the war lasted, the more serious it became for German civilians. By 1918 the German people were nearly starving. They were living on a diet of potatoes and sawdusty bread. To feed their animals, farmers would go round the town collecting food waste. In the colder months of late 1917 and early 1918, a shortage of fuel led to many people dying of cold. In this situation, mothers would go to any lengths to keep their children warm.

4. How far do **Sources C** and **D** agree about the problems faced by people in Germany in 1918?

4

[End of Context IIA]

Marks

UNIT III – PEOPLE AND POWER

CONTEXT D: GERMANY 1918–1939

SECTION A: KNOWLEDGE AND UNDERSTANDING

**Study the information in the sources. You must also use your own
information in your answers.**

Source A is from *Hitler: Military Commander* by Rupert Matthews.

Source A

> In 1923 Hitler launched a Nazi coup in Bavaria. The aim was to replace the
> civilian government with one led by Hitler. The Nazi Stormtroopers seized
> key government buildings while Hitler announced his take over of power in a
> meeting room in a cellar. The march was brought to a bloody halt by the hail of
> gunfire from police marksmen. Hitler was arrested and briefly imprisoned. The
> coup was crucial to Hitler's relationship with the army. He had on his side Erich
> Ludendorff, the highly respected First World War leader.

1. How important was the Beer Hall Putsch in the Nazi Party's rise to power?   **4**

Source B is a photograph of the inside of a Jewish Synagogue in Berlin after
'Kristallnacht', November 9–10th 1938.

Source B

2. What methods did Hitler use to persecute Jewish people in Germany, up to
   1939?   **3**

Marks

SECTION B: ENQUIRY SKILLS

The following sources are about discontent with the Weimar Republic and the coming to power of the Nazi Party.

Study the sources carefully and answer the questions which follow.
You should use your own knowledge where appropriate.

Source C from *Weimar Germany and the Rise of the Nazis* by Stephen Burant.

Source C

> To many Germans, National Socialism offered a more successful way of governing the country. After the financial collapse in the years following 1929, the Weimar Republic was doomed. The Nazi party took full advantage of the economic depression. The Nazis launched a large scale propaganda campaign, and won a mass following. Nazi ideas which promised a social revolution, appealed particularly to German youth, who longed for the restoration of order.

3. To what extent does **Source C** explain why the Weimar Republic collapsed? 4

Source D was written by a supporter of the Nazis.

Source D

> In 1933 only one party offered a promise of better things. National Socialism seemed to offer a solution to the suffering caused by the economic depression and the unemployment which followed it. The Nazi troopers, in their smart uniforms, seemed to present a picture of order, after the unrest surrounding the weakness of the Weimar Republic. Nazi newspapers and rallies all seemed to offer a more stable government.

4. To what extent do **Sources C** and **D** agree on why the Nazis came to power in 1933?

Source E was written by *Daily Express* journalist, Seftan Delmer, on February 23rd 1933. 4

Source E

> The fire broke out at 9.45 tonight in the Reichstag building. Five minutes later, I was outside the Reichstag watching the flames. I suddenly saw the famous black motor car of Adolf Hitler slide past. I rushed after Hitler and entered the Reichstag. Hitler turned to me and said. "This is a God-given opportunity. This is the work of the Communists. You are going to witness the beginning of a great new period in German history." I do not believe this. They are blaming the Communists to give them an excuse to ban their party and impose dictatorship.

5. What does the author of **Source E** think about the Reichstag Fire? 3

[End of Context IIID]

[End of question paper]

Exam A – Credit Level

History

Standard Grade: Credit

Practice Papers
For SQA Exams

Exam A
Credit Level

You are allowed 1 hour and 45 minutes to complete this exam.

Answer all questions from all three Units.

Choose only **one** Context from each Unit, then answer the questions in **both** Section A **and** Section B (Knowledge & Understanding **and** Enquiry Skills). **Please note this book only contains Contexts Unit IB, Unit IIA and Unit IIID as these are the most popular units in Scottish Schools.**

The complete list of Contexts in this exam is shown below:

Use information from the sources and your own studies in your answers.

Some sources have been changed to meet the needs of this exam.

Leckie × Leckie
Scotland's leading educational publishers

Marks

UNIT I – CHANGING LIFE IN SCOTLAND AND BRITAIN

CONTEXT B 1830s–1930s

SECTION A: KNOWLEDGE AND UNDERSTANDING

During the nineteenth and early-twentieth century, many Irish immigrated to Scotland and had a great impact on the country.

1. Explain the impact of Irish immigration on Scotland.   **3**

The British Government started to influence improvements in Coal Mining, including passing the 1842 Coal Mines Act.

2. How important was the Coal Mines Act of 1842 in improving mine safety?   **4**

Marks

SECTION B: ENQUIRY SKILLS

The issue for investigating is:

The Suffragettes used the correct methods in their campaign to get Votes for Women from 1903 to 1914.

**Study the sources carefully and answer the questions which follow.
You should use your own knowledge where appropriate.**

Source A is from a letter written by Emmeline Pankhurst to a Scottish Suffragette.

Source A

> January 10th 1913
>
> My Dear Friend
>
> The Prime Minister has announced that the Women's Amendments to the Manhood Suffrage Bill will shortly be discussed in Parliament. The WSPU has declined to call any truce on its militant activities on the strength of the Prime Minister's promise to discuss the issue of votes for women. There is no commitment from the government to get the act carried. We must continue to show our determination. Women have been disappointed in the past. We will fight on and cause as much public disorder as we can. The cause is a just cause and it will triumph.

3. How useful is **Source A** for investigating the Suffragette movement in the period 1903 to 1914?

4

Source B is from the *Haddingtonshire Courier*, March 6th 1914.

Source B

> Outrage! The most daring Suffragette militancy occurred at an early hour last Friday morning. The beautiful medieval church of Whitekirk, one of the most valued ecclesiastical treasures in Scotland, was burned to the ground. On examining the building, the police found a hammer and a knife wrapped in paper on which was written: "By torturing the finest and noblest women in the country, you are driving more into rebellion. Stop forcible feeding! No surrender."

Source C is from a letter written by the President of a Women's Liberal Association in 1912.

Source C

> We wish to protest against the illegal actions of the members of the Women's Social and Political Union. While sympathising with their cause, we feel deeply that their militancy is not only a disgrace to the women concerned but also the gravest hindrance to the cause of Woman's suffrage. We wish to point out to the Liberal Government that the numbers involved are of no account compared to the women who use constitutional methods to get the vote. I am, yours truly, Eva McLaren.

Look at Sources A, B and C.

4. What evidence in the sources supports the view that the Suffragettes used the correct methods in their campaign to get Votes for Women?

    What evidence in the sources does **not** support the view that Suffragettes used the correct methods in their campaign to get Votes for Women? **6**

5. How far do you agree that the Suffragettes, from 1903 to 1914, used the correct methods in their campaign to get Votes for Women? **5**

You should use evidence **from the sources** and **your own knowledge** to reach a **balanced conclusion**.

[End of Context IB]

Marks

UNIT II – INTERNATIONAL CONFLICT AND COOPERATION

CONTEXT A 1890s–1920s

SECTION A: KNOWLEDGE AND UNDERSTANDING

On the outbreak of war in 1914, British politician Sir Edward Gray commented, "The lights are going out all over Europe and I doubt we will see them go on again in our lifetime."

1. How important as a cause of World War One was:

    EITHER

    a) imperial rivalries?　　　　　　　　　　　　　　　　　　　　　　　**8**

    　　　OR

    b) nationalism in the Balkans?　　　　　　　　　　　　　　　　　　　**8**

SECTION B: ENQUIRY SKILLS

The following sources are about the effects of trench warfare on soldiers on the Western Front.

Study the sources carefully and answer the questions which follow.
You should use your own knowledge where appropriate.

Source A was drawn by Ernest Thompson in the summer of 1916.

Source A

"Gee, Bill. These trenches won't be as nice as this in the winter."

2. Discuss the attitude of the author of **Source A** towards conditions in the trenches during World War One.　　　　　　　　　　　　　　　　　　　**3**

Source B was written by Fusilier Victor Packer.

> When I got out to the front in 1916 I wondered what the devil I'd got into. It was nothing but mud and filth. All the chaps who were already there looked like tramps, all plastered with filth and dirt. It didn't take long for the bottom of my overcoat to get just as sodden. It was impossible to keep things clean, even your most important possessions – your Lee Enfield rifle and bayonet.

3. How far do **Sources A** and **B** agree about trench conditions on the Western Front?   **5**

Source C was said by Private Underwood who was involved in the first gas attack in 1915.

Source C

> As we looked, we saw this green cloud come slowly over the terrain. One of our boys, evidently a chemist, passed the word that this was chlorine. And he said 'If you urinate on your handkerchief and hold it over your nose, it will save your lungs, anyway.' So most of us did that. There were masses of Germans behind the gas cloud, we could see their grey uniforms as plain as anything.

4. How fully does **Source C** describe a gas attack in World War One?   **4**

You must use evidence **from the source** and **your own knowledge** and give reasons for your answer.

[End of Context IIA]

Marks

UNIT III – PEOPLE AND POWER

CONTEXT D: GERMANY 1918–1939

SECTION A: KNOWLEDGE AND UNDERSTANDING

Throughout the 1920s the Weimar Government in Germany had many problems, some of them of their own making.

1. Describe the failings of the Weimar Republic in the 1920s.   3

On the evening of 27 February 1933, the German Parliament (the Reichstag) was on fire. Hitler was quick to attend the scene.

2. Explain in what ways the Reichstag Fire was used by the Nazis.   4

SECTION B: ENQUIRY SKILLS

The following sources are about the Hitler Youth.

**Study the sources carefully and answer the questions which follow.
You should use your own knowledge where appropriate.**

Source C is a poster produced in Germany in the mid 1930s. The German words say "Officers of tomorrow".

Source A

3.   How useful is **Source A** as evidence of the appeal of Nazi youth groups?   **4**

Source B is from *The Third Reich: A New History* by Michael Burleigh.

Source B

> Viewed superficially, the Hitler Youth seems very like a version of the prohibited Boy Scouts, with a similar emphasis upon competition and drill. There was also great stress put on uniformed team work. However, there was a much greater military agenda including training in marksmanship and weaponry. Sports such as boxing and other tough pursuits concentrated the young on preparation for the army.

4.   To what extent do **Sources A** and **B** agree about the Hitler Youth?   **5**

[End of Context IIID]

[End of question paper]

Exam B – Credit Level

History   Standard Grade: Credit

Practice Papers   **Exam B**
For SQA Exams   **Credit Level**

You are allowed 1 hour and 45 minutes to complete this exam.

Answer all questions from all three Units.

Choose only **one** Context from each Unit, then answer the questions in **both** Section A **and** Section B (Knowledge & Understanding **and** Enquiry Skills). **Please note this book only contains Contexts Unit IB, Unit IIA and Unit IIID as these are the most popular units in Scottish Schools.**

The complete list of Contexts in this exam is shown below:

      Unit I – Changing Life in Scotland and Britain
          Context B: 1830s–1930s   **Pages 80–82**

      Unit II – International Conflict and Cooperation
          Context A: 1890s–1920s   **Pages 83–84**

      Unit III – People and Power
          Context D: Germany 1918–1939   **Pages 85–86**

Use information from the sources and your own studies in your answers.

Some sources have been changed to meet the needs of this exam.

Scotland's leading educational publishers

Marks

UNIT I – CHANGING LIFE IN SCOTLAND AND BRITAIN

CONTEXT B 1830s–1930s

SECTION A: KNOWLEDGE AND UNDERSTANDING

Scottish emigrants moved to countries all across the world and had a great impact wherever they went.

1. Describe the lives of Scotland's emigrants overseas.

4

Building railway lines was not easy and a number of solutions had to be found before building could start.

2. Explain some of the problems in building the railways in Scotland.

3

SECTION B: ENQUIRY SKILLS

The issue for investigating is:

Housing in Scotland improved dramatically in the late nineteenth and early twentieth centuries.

Study the sources carefully and answer the questions which follow. You should use your own knowledge where appropriate.

Source A from a report made following the Census of 1911.

Source A

> It is now possible to produce some summaries based on the evidence of the Census held in Scotland on April 2nd 1911. Very few homes have been reported possessing no windows. The number of people living in one room homes has dropped to 13% of the total. However, the number of people living in two roomed homes is still high at 41%. Almost half of all Scots live at a density of more than two people per room. The figure in England is just 7%. In the great cities, the situation is worse. There are over 44,000 homes in Glasgow where the inhabitants share a toilet. Housing conditions are much better in the smaller burghs.

3. How useful is **Source A** for investigating housing in early-twentieth century Scotland?

4

Source B is from *Farm Life in Northeast Scotland* by Ian Carter.

Source B

> A typical farm cottage in Buchan in the middle of the nineteenth century had side walls barely five feet (1.5 metres) in height. The door was so low an ordinary sized person, on entering, required to bend considerably. The gables were built with turfs. The stone work was composed of rough surface stone and mortar. The roof was covered with turfs, overlaid with straw. The floor was just the bare earth. By 1880, there was some improvement, especially in the better off ploughman's cottages but in many cases conditions remained unaltered.

Source C is from *Changing Lives, Scotland and Britain* by Sydney Wood.

Source C

> Housing Acts in the 1920s and 1930s did something to improve living conditions in Scotland. The government helped local authorities with the cost of council house building. The government also encouraged private house building.
> In the 1930s, people began to buy their own, well built homes with proper amenities. Much was done, yet many people were still far from well housed when the outbreak of the Second World War put an end to new house building. Overcrowding in the city slums was still far worse than in England. In the countryside, many men still lived in inadequate bothies.

Look at Sources A, B and C.

4. What evidence is there in the sources to support the view that housing in Scotland was improving?

   What evidence in the sources **does not** support the view that housing in Scotland was improving?   **6**

5. How far do you agree with the view that housing in Scotland improved dramatically in the late nineteenth and early twentieth centuries?   **5**

   You must use **evidence from the sources** and **your own knowledge** to reach a **balanced conclusion.**

[End of Context IB]

Marks

UNIT II – INTERNATIONAL CONFLICT AND COOPERATION

CONTEXT A 1890s–1920s

SECTION A: KNOWLEDGE AND UNDERSTANDING

> As well as winning battles, it was vital that the allies kept good order and discipline both on the battlefield at home if they were to win the war.

1. How important as a cause of allied casualties in World War One was:

    EITHER

    a) poor tactics used by commanders? **8**

    OR

    b) disease in the trenches? **8**

SECTION B: ENQUIRY SKILLS

The following sources are about the experiences of war on civilians in Britain.

Study the sources carefully and answer the questions which follow.

You should use your own knowledge where appropriate.

Source A is from *All Quiet on the Home Front* by historian Richard Van Emden. It was published in 2003.

Source A

> The press and the government were in a quandary about Zeppelin attacks on British towns. They could not decide whether to highlight them in order to condemn the killing of women and children, or to keep such reports low key for fear of fuelling public anxiety. The Defence of the Realm Act included restrictions on the press, forbidding the reporting of news liable to cause alarm and despondency. Yet, when the first attack over London took place on 31st May 1915, the *Daily News* ran the front page headline "Zeppelin Raid Over Outer London".

2. How useful is **Source A** as evidence of life in Britain during World War One? **4**

Marks

Source B is from the memoirs of Margery Porter who lived in London in 1915–16.

Source B

> There were quite a few Zeppelin raids. We all lived in flats where there was a long passage at the bottom and all the people from the three storeys above us used to come down and there we all sat, in some anxiety. I wouldn't say people were really frightened. It was just the suspense of the unknown. Some would say "Oh dear, let's hope this soon goes over." This was the first time we'd had bombs on London. I think people were a bit awe-struck. War had never been like this before. My father was a Special Constable and he had to go round making sure people had their curtains pulled tight.

3. Discuss the attitude of the author of **Source B** towards air raids.   3

4. How fully do **Sources A** and **B** describe how the war affected the lives of British civilians?   5

   You must use evidence **from the source** and **your own knowledge** and give reasons for your answer.

[End of Context IIA]

Marks

UNIT III – PEOPLE AND POWER

CONTEXT D: GERMANY 1918–1939

SECTION A: KNOWLEDGE AND UNDERSTANDING

After the war the victorious leaders met at Versailles to decide Germany's fate.
---

1.   How important was the Treaty of Versailles in causing problems for the Weimar
     Republic in the 1920s?   **3**

Hitler became leader of Germany in 1934 and called himself Fuhrer.
---

2.   Explain in what ways Hitler gained power by 1934.   **4**

SECTION B: ENQUIRY SKILLS

The following sources are about education for girls in Nazi Germany.

**Study the sources carefully and answer the questions which follow.
You should use your own knowledge where appropriate.**

Source A is from a speech made by Joseph Goebbels in 1933.

Source A

> At the risk of sounding outdated, let me say this clearly. We must teach our children that the first, best, and most suitable place for women is in the family. A woman's duty is to give children to her nation. The woman is the teacher of the youth, and therefore the builder of the foundation of the future. We must educate all girls to realise that the best place for a woman to serve her people is in the motherhood of the German nation. This is her real task – leave working to men. Girls should not try to fill the roles of men. Girls must be taught to dress correctly for their role.

3. Discuss the attitude of the writer of **Source A** towards education for girls.   4

Source B is a poster produced by the Nazis in the mid 1930s. The German words say: "Support the National Effort. Mother and child."

Source B

4. To what extent does **Source A** agree with **Source B** about how the Nazis believed girls should be educated?   5

[End of Context IIID]

[End of question paper]

Exam C – Credit Level

History   Standard Grade: Credit

Practice Papers   Exam C
For SQA Exams   Credit Level

You are allowed 1 hour and 45 minutes to complete this exam.

Answer all questions from all three Units.

Choose only **one** Context from each Unit, then answer the questions in **both** Section A **and** Section B (Knowledge & Understanding **and** Enquiry Skills). **Please note this book only contains Contexts Unit IB, Unit IIA and Unit IIID as these are the most popular units in Scottish Schools.**

The complete list of Contexts in this exam is shown below:

   Unit I – Changing Life in Scotland and Britain
      Context B: 1830s–1930s   **Pages 90–91**

   Unit II – International Conflict and Cooperation
      Context A: 1890s–1920s   **Pages 92–93**

   Unit III – People and Power
      Context D: Germany 1918–1939   **Page 94**

Use information from the sources and your own studies in your answers.

Some sources have been changed to meet the needs of this exam.

Leckie×Leckie
Scotland's leading educational publishers

UNIT I – CHANGING LIFE IN SCOTLAND AND BRITAIN

Marks

CONTEXT B 1830s–1930s

SECTION A: KNOWLEDGE AND UNDERSTANDING

By 1930 coal mines were safer places to work, as a result of a range of measures introduced for the benefit of miners.
---

1. How important in improving safety in coal mines between 1830 and 1930 was:

   EITHER

   a) government action   **8**

   OR

   b) new technology?   **8**

SECTION B: ENQUIRY SKILLS

The issue for investigating is: Emigration from Scotland between 1840 and 1930 was disastrous for the emigrants.

Study the sources carefully and answer the questions which follow. You should use your own knowledge where appropriate.

Source A was written by history professor Rosalind Michison in *A History of Scotland*, published in 1993.

Source A

In some areas, moving the peasantry from the land in the Highlands was done with consideration and skill. In much of south Argyll the population found other activities. In other areas, the change was brutal. The argument about how many left Scotland voluntarily and how many were forced to emigrate still goes on. Life in early-nineteenth century Scotland was tough for those without property. The density of population in some areas meant that the standard of living was appallingly low. In all probability, some three times as many people left the Highlands of their own free will as from direct eviction.
---

2. How useful is **Source A** for investigating emigration from Scotland in the nineteenth century?   **4**

Source B is from an eyewitness account from Catherine MacPhee of Barra.

Source B

> I saw our houses swept away and the people being driven out of the countryside to the streets of Glasgow and to the wilds of Canada, such as them that did not die of hunger and smallpox while going across the ocean. I have seen the women putting their children in the carts which were being sent from Benbecula to board an emigrant ship on Loch Boisdale. Almost everyone was crying. Bailiffs and constables gathered behind them and made sure they boarded the ship. Some men showed boldness and looked for adventure but for most it was a loathsome day.

Source C is from *The Scottish Nation* by T. Devine.

Source C

> Over 2 million Scots emigrated between the 1820s and the First World War – a huge percentage of the population. All areas of Scotland were affected – it was associated with areas of economic growth as well as regions of economic decline. The popularity of destinations varied over time: Canada, Australia, New Zealand, United States. It would be nonsense to assume that all succeeded in their new country. However, many thrived and the record of the emigrant Scots in the making of North America and Australasia is a formidable one.

Look at Sources A, B, and C

3. What evidence is there in the sources to support the view that emigration was a disaster for emigrants from Scotland?

   What evidence in the sources disagrees with the view that emigration was a disaster for emigrants from Scotland?   **6**

4. How far do you agree that emigration from Scotland between 1840 and 1930 was disastrous for the emigrants?   **5**

   You must use **evidence from the sources** and **your own knowledge** to reach a **balanced conclusion**.

[End of Context IB]

Marks

UNIT II – INTERNATIONAL CONFLICT AND COOPERATION

CONTEXT A 1890s–1920s

SECTION A: KNOWLEDGE AND UNDERSTANDING

> By 1914 Europe was at war following years of tension and rivalries.

1. Describe the tensions between the Great Powers in Europe at the start of the twentieth century?

    4

> The League of Nations was the brainchild of US President Woodrow Wilson. It was one of his 'Fourteen Points' at the end of the First World War.

2. How successful was the League of Nations in achieving its aims in the 1920s?

    4

SECTION B: ENQUIRY SKILLS

The following sources are about the end of the war and the resulting Treaty of Versailles.

Study the sources carefully and answer the questions which follow.

You should use your own knowledge where appropriate.

Source A is from www.firstworldwar.com

Source A

> On 4 July 1918, General Monash launched an attack by unleashing a co-ordinated barrage of tanks, artillery and warplanes, all designed to clear a path for advancing infantry. Monash saw no point in attempting to gain ground by using infantry to storm enemy machine gun positions. He believed in using new technology, with tanks at the forefront. Tanks were increasingly used during the Allied advance of 1918 and reached a grand scale, when 604 Allied tanks assisted a twenty mile advance. Major General Fuller's plan involving a massive use of tanks for an offensive was never used, because Germany surrendered.

3. How accurately does **Source A** describe the role of the tank in World War One?

    4

Marks

Source B is from an editorial in a Dutch newspaper in June 1919.

Source B

> We understand the bitter feelings of the Entente countries. However, the peace conditions imposed upon Germany are so hard that those who expected a "peace of justice" are bound to be deeply disappointed. Everybody knows how we condemned the crimes committed against humanity by Germany: the invasion of Belgium; the use of poison gas; the Zeppelin raids on innocent civilians. However, this must not amount to a lasting condemnation of a whole people. The financial burden is so heavy that Germany is reduced to economic bondage.

4. Discuss the attitude of the author of **Source B** towards the Treaty of Versailles. **4**

Source C is from a speech by Georges Clemenceau in June 1919.

Source C

> The Germans are responsible for the savage manner in which the war was conducted. The rulers of Germany violated the neutrality of Belgium. They were the first to use poisonous gas, notwithstanding the appalling suffering it entailed. They began the bombing of towns solely for the purpose of reducing morale by striking at women and children. There must be harsh justice for the dead and wounded. We insist that Germany must undertake to make financial reparation to the very uttermost of her power.

5. How far do **Sources B** and **C** agree about the treatment of Germany at Versailles? **5**

[End of Context IIA]

Marks

UNIT III – PEOPLE AND POWER

CONTEXT D: GERMANY 1918–1939

SECTION A: KNOWLEDGE AND UNDERSTANDING

The Weimar Government emerged in Germany following World War One and gave German people a democratic system of rule.
---

1. Why did many Germans dislike the Weimar Government in the 1920s?   **3**

The Nazi State came down hard on opposition groups in Germany using whatever means necessary.
---

2. Describe some attempts to oppose Nazi rule between 1934 and 1939.   **4**

SECTION B: ENQUIRY SKILLS

The following sources are about the characteristics of the National Socialist Government.

Study the sources carefully and answer the questions which follow. You should use your own knowledge where appropriate.

Source A comes from a booklet produced for Hitler Youth leaders in 1937.

Source A

It is dangerous for the existence of a pure race to mix with foreign blood. Racial hygiene means a defence against the corruption of our blood by the Jews. The Jewish dominance in aspects of life over the last decades has shown all Germans the destructive and corrupting nature of this people. National Socialism's first defensive measures therefore were aimed at driving the Jews out of our people's cultural and economic life. Numerous laws have created the foundation for this.
---

3. How useful is **Source A** as evidence of Nazi attitudes towards Jewish people?   **4**

Source B is a website definition of National Socialism.

Source B

Nazism brought together the ideas of Social Darwinism (that certain individuals or ethnic groups are dominant because of their inherent genetic superiority), and Lebensraum (the belief that Germans needed more 'living space' particularly in Eastern Europe). Nazism also embraced the attitude of total anti-Bolshevism, and demanded revenge against those people who, they claimed, had 'betrayed' Germany during World War I and caused it to be vanquished by the enemy.
---

4. How fully do **Sources A** and **B** describe the aims of the Nazi Party in Germany between 1933 and 1939?   **5**

    You must use evidence **from the source** and **your own knowledge**.

[End of Context IIID]

[End of question paper]

Answers

Remember that Section One gives you a lot of good advice on how to answer each question type, both in Knowledge and Understanding (KU) and Enquiry Skills (ES).

When you have tried some of the sample exam papers you should then turn to this answers section. The aim of answers is to give you a very clear idea of the kind of information that a marker will be looking for when marking Standard Grade General and Credit History exams. The answers are provided here as bullet points so that you can see quickly and easily a wide selection of acceptable ideas. This is **not** the way in which you should write your answers. You must always write in complete sentences, **similar to the sample answers from Tom and Amy in Section One of the booklet.**

The only exception to this rule is if you wish to present a chart in your response to the 'select and organise evidence' (ES5) type of question.

The answers in this booklet represent some of the possible information that you could put in your answers. However, in History there are often many more answers to each of the questions. As long as your facts are accurate, relevant to the question and used to correctly address the question, you will be given credit.

Unit I, Context B

1.

> **See page 11 for more help.**　KU1 (out of 3 marks). Remember that to get full marks you must have at least one piece of remembered information in your answer.

The **evidence from the source** about new technology used in mines is:

- steam engines dragged coal to the surface
- steam engines powered the safety cages

Other possible evidence about new technology includes:

- the Davy safety lamp was introduced
- wire was developed instead of rope for lifting cages with heavier loads
- iron cages were introduced for lifting and lowering miners
- electric fans ventilated mines by the twentieth century
- iron props were used instead of wooden props
- electric powered cutting equipment was introduced
- electric conveyor belts were used
- electric lighting was put in
- wagon ways and small train systems were used underground
- steam and later electric powered pumps were used to remove water

2.

See page 14 for more help. KU2 (out of 4 marks). Remember that to get full marks you must have at least one piece of remembered information in your answer.

The **evidence from the source** explaining why the population went up is:

- better medical care produced a decline in the death rate
- medical improvements contributed to falling mortality
- improved living standards reduced the number of deaths

Other possible evidence about the reasons for population rise includes:

- the discovery of the link between dirty water and disease led to better sanitation which prolonged life
- a better diet led to longer living
- new medicines such as penicillin and antibiotics helped prolong life
- better housing and sanitation contributed to better health and hence longer living
- immigrants came to Scotland from a variety of countries, boosting the population figures

3.

See page 19 for more help. ES1 (out of 3 marks). Remember to state whether the source is useful or of limited use.

Source C is useful for investigating 19th century railway development because:

- it is a primary source written at the time (of railway development) {contemporaneity}
- it is an official, government record (of Parliament) {authorship}
- it gives details of railway development/government attitude to railways {content}
- it is a true account, matching your own (**and given**) knowledge {accuracy}
- it is an accurate record of debates in parliament {purpose}
- however, it is just one piece of evidence/ recording one MP's view {limitation}

4.

See page 30 for more help. ES5 (out of 5 marks). A maximum of three marks can be awarded if the relevant evidence is selected for only one side of the issue.

Evidence for the issue, from Source C:

- railways brought benefits to poor/neglected areas
- they helped crofters/ farmers
- they promoted fishing interests (in W. Highlands)

Evidence against the issue, from Source D:

- railways altered the landscape (dramatically)
- Forth Rail Bridge had huge impact
- Tay Bridge collapsed
- people lost lives through railway disasters

5.

See page 30 for more help. ES6 (out of 4 marks). A conclusion which takes account of one side only and/or is based solely on either presented evidence or recall can be awarded a maximum of two marks.

A good, balanced conclusion is reached using **presented evidence** such as that listed above, and also **at least one point of recalled information such as:**

possible points <u>for the issue</u>

- railways offered cheap travel
- the coal industry benefited from the railways
- agriculture benefited
- the newspaper industry benefited
- railways gave new employment opportunities: on the railways; building railways
- the iron and steel industries were boosted
- the tourist trade was boosted
- railways provided opportunities for travel/ holidays/ commuting
- fresh food could be delivered quicker by rail
- fishermen could get transport fresh fish by rail
- mail/newspapers could be delivered efficiently on the railways

possible points <u>against the issue:</u>

- stage coaches became obsolete
- the canal industry declined
- road engineers lost jobs
- toll operators were affected
- railways caused environmental issues
- railways made farmers worried about effect on livestock
- there were complaints about Sunday travel
- some doctors feared the effects of rail travel on peoples' health

---

Unit II, Context A

1.

See page 15 for more help. KU3 (out of 3 marks). Remember that to get full marks you must have at least one piece of remembered information in your answer.

The **evidence from the source** about the importance of nationalist feelings in the Balkans in causing World War One is:

- Slavs competed with each other from the start
- independence did not end the problems in this area

Other possible evidence about the causes of World War One includes:

- nationalist rivalries spilled over with the assassinations of Franz Ferdinand and his wife by Gavrilo Princip
- Alliances contributed to the war, turning a minor conflict into a full scale war
- naval rivalries had caused tension
- the arms race had caused tension
- there were existing tensions between European powers over Empires
- the German invasion of Belgium / Treaty of London caused Britain to join the war

2.

See page 11 for more help. KU1 (out of 4 marks). Remember that to get full marks you must have at least one piece of remembered information in your answer.

The **evidence from the source** about the difficulties soldiers faced is:

- mud would drag off a man's boots
- men have to be hauled out of mud using ropes
- the weather was beastly

Other possible evidence about the difficulties facing soldiers includes:

- rats would eat food, gnaw soldiers' faces and spread disease
- standing in water (flooding) could cause trench foot
- poor sanitary conditions could cause dysentery
- constant artillery bombardment could cause shell shock
- many soldiers were killed or injured by artillery, machine gun fire/ snipers
- gas attacks caused serious injuries and death
- many soldiers suffered from boredom on the front lines
- soldiers had to try and keep awake on sentry duty

3.

See page 28 for more help. ES4 (out of 3 marks). Remember that to get full marks, you must have at least one piece of evidence from the source and at least one piece of remembered information in your answer.

The **evidence given in Source C** about why young men joined the British army is:

- to fight the Germans
- to show the Germans they meant business
- to fulfil expectations/ prove their bravery/manhood
- to teach the Germans a lesson
- to be a soldier/ to get into the uniform

Other possible evidence why men joined up includes:

- for patriotic reasons (King and Country)
- to avenge the invasion of Belgium
- for adventure/excitement
- out of peer pressure
- to impress/protect women
- to avoid accusations of cowardice (getting a white feather)

4.

See page 23 for more help. ES2 (out of 4 marks). Remember that you get one mark for a simple comparison (marked*) and two marks for a developed comparison.

Here are some of the ways in which the sources agree:

*The Sources agree that the war would be like a game/an adventure:

Source C says   play the greater game

Source D says: it would be fun/a great game/come back with the trophy

*The Sources agree that men volunteered to fight the Germans:

Source C says/shows: Germans said you wouldn't come/men shooting (Germans)

Source D says: we would beat the Germans

*The Sources agree that men liked the (khaki) uniform/cap

Source C shows: men in army uniform

Source D says: we all wanted the uniform

*The Sources agree that men were angry at being called cissies (cowards)

Source C says: Germans said you were not in earnest

Source D says: Germans said we were not brave enough to come and fight

5.

See page 26 for more help. ES3 (out of 3 marks). Remember to discuss the author's attitude to the event or issue.

The attitude of the author about fighting in the war is that he was:

• feeling cheerful about it
• happier than for many months
• confident of success
• depressed at the many losses (deaths)
• missing his comrades
• consoled that men are dying in a good cause

Unit III, Context D

1.

See page 14 for more help. KU2 (out of 3 marks). Remember that to get full marks you must have at least one piece of remembered information in your answer.

The **evidence from the source** explaining in what ways the Ruhr Crisis caused the collapse of the Weimar Government is:

• extremist groups exploited the crisis to their advantage
• in Saxony and Thuringia, Communists worked to lay the basis for a more socialist government
• Communist uprisings happened in Hamburg

Other possible evidence why the Weimar Government collapsed includes:

- many lost faith in Weimar due to their poor decisions/lack of leadership
- many were upset that the Weimar government had let Belgian and French troops invade German soil
- many upset at problems caused by hyperinflation
- many Germans lost jobs as a result of the crisis and so lost faith in Weimar
- the Ruhr Crisis caused instability that gave hope to the Nazis in their attack on Munich in 1924

2.

> *See page 15 for more help.*   KU3 (out of 4 marks). Remember that to get full marks you must have at least one piece of remembered information in your answer.

The **evidence from the source** used to assess the importance of Hitler's promise of jobs in him gaining popularity is that:

- workers were fearful of the future and turned to the Nazis
- the Nazis made promises to reduce unemployment
- social and cultural factors also accounted for Nazi appeal

Other possible evidence explaining why Hitler became popular includes:

- Hitler also promised to rip up the Treaty of Versailles
- Hitler also promised to make Germany strong again
- Hitler restored German pride by rebuilding her armed forces
- Hitler set up public work schemes
- propaganda increased Hitler's popularity in all area
- terror was used to ensure any opposition was crushed

3.

> *See page 19 for more help.*   ES1 (out of 4 marks). Remember to state whether the source is useful or of limited use.

Source C is useful as evidence of Nazi methods of control because:

- it is a primary source written at the time (of the Nazis in control) {contemporaneity}
- it was written by a German journalist with first hand information {authorship}
- it gives good information about the setting up of a concentration camp {content}
- it is a true account matching your own evidence **which you must give** {accuracy}
- it was written to give information to newspaper readers {purpose}
- however, it is a journalistic account and may be biased {limitation}

4.

See page 23 for more help. ES2 (out of 4 marks). Remember that you get one mark for a simple comparison (marked*) and two marks for a developed comparison.

Here are some of the ways in which the sources agree or disagree:

*The Sources agree that Communists were arrested:

Source C says: all Communist (criminals) will be arrested

Source D says: Communist (opponents) arrested by the police

*The Sources agree that the Nazi police arrested Communists:

Source C says: arrested by the police or Gestapo

Source D says: arrested by the police forces

*The Sources agree that Communists were taken to a concentration camp:

Source C says: Communists will be assembled in…concentration camp

Source D says: sent to a concentration camp

*The Sources agree that Communists had little choice/no real hope of justice:

Source C says: not appropriate to let them go free/reassure the population

Source D says: they were beaten until they agreed to go

*The Sources disagree about their chances of release:

Source C says: protective custody would not go on any longer than necessary

Source D says: you were released when authorities thought fit – this rarely happened

and also:

*Only Source D says that Communists had to 'learn their lesson' – i.e. be retrained.

Answers	General Paper B

Unit I, Context B

1.

See page 11 for more help. KU1 (out of 3 marks). Remember that to get full marks you must have at least one piece of remembered information in your answer.

The **evidence from the source** describing the methods used by Suffragists is:

- they would write magazines and newspapers
- they would organise and write speeches

Other possible evidence of what Suffragists did includes:

- they wrote letters to Members of Parliament
- they organised petitions and sent them to parliament
- they held peaceful processions and marches
- they prepared and handed out posters and leaflets

2.

See page 14 for more help. KU2 (out of 4 marks). Remember that to get full marks you must have at least one piece of remembered information in your answer.

The evidence **from the source** which explains why railways brought benefits to the people in Scottish towns is:

- large numbers were carried to work by rail
- large numbers were taken to school by rail
- railways took people to entertainment and back home again

Other possible evidence explaining why railways brought benefits includes:

- people in towns could now get fresh food delivered by rail
- people in towns could now get daily national newspapers by rail
- businesses prospered as businessmen could sell goods further away and buy goods from across Britain
- new businesses and employment came about as a result of the railways
- Football Leagues became national and supporters travelled across the country to watch their team
- time in all towns became standardised (GMT) with the coming of railways

3.

See page 19 for more help. ES1 (out of 3 marks). Remember to state whether the source is useful or of limited use.

Source C is useful for investigating conditions in nineteenth century coal mines because:

- it is a primary source written at the time (of nineteenth century mining conditions) {contemporaneity}
- it is an eyewitness account {authorship}
- it gives useful information about mining conditions {content}
- it is a true account matching your own (**and given**) evidence {accuracy}

- it was written to make an accurate report on young people in mines {purpose}
- however, it is just one piece of evidence recording one view/in one area {limitation}

4.

| See page 30 for more help. | ES5 (out of 5 marks). A maximum of three marks can be awarded if the relevant evidence is selected for only one side of the issue. |

Evidence for the issue, from Source C:

- the picture shows a girl harnessed to a tub
- nowhere else do people work like this
- incredible that human beings can do such work
- (miners went) crawling on hands and knees
- (the girl/coal miner) was dragging a tub full of coal/ up a slope
- (she) works in the dark
- (she) has to eat down the mine

Evidence against the issue, from Source D:

- the collier had pride in his work
- colliers had position in society (on account of his strength)
- coal miners used great skill
- colliers were their own bosses/more independent
- no one told them what to do
- their wages went up

5.

| See page 30 for more help. | ES6 (out of 5 marks). A conclusion which takes account of one side only and/or is based solely on either presented evidence or recall can be awarded a maximum of two marks. |

A good, balanced conclusion is reached using **presented evidence** such as that listed above, and also **at least one point of recalled information such as:**

Possible points for the issue:

- very young children worked as trappers/putters
- coal mining was very dangerous
- colliers could be killed by explosion from gas
- cave ins/flooding occurred
- inefficient/dangerous methods were used to get down the pit
- the work was very hard
- lungs were affected by dust
- colliers worked long hours
- miners worked in wet conditions
- children in the mines got little chance of schooling
- there was a possibility of dying young
- miners suffered from deprivation of daylight/ vitamin D
- there was harsh discipline/ children were beaten
- even with new machinery, conditions were hard
- new coal cutting machinery brought problems (e.g. dust)

Possible points against the issue:

- 1842 Act stopped women and children working underground
- other Acts improved conditions

- wagonways were constructed to move coal
- steam and electrical power was used to raise wire rope cages
- steam and electrical drainage pumps came in
- safety lamp/lighting helped avoid explosions
- ventilation fans helped
- metal or concrete pit props were used to prevent collapse
- electrical coal cutting/conveyor belts brought improvements
- mining was better than the hard, boring work in a cotton mill
- mining was better than farm gang work

Unit II, Context A

1.

See page 15 for more help. | KU3 (out of 3 marks). Remember that to get full marks you must have at least one piece of remembered information in your answer.

Evidence from the source assessing the importance of propaganda in encouraging men to join the army is:

- the poster said that their King and Country needed them
- men were swept up in a wave of patriotism, brought about by propaganda
- men joined to escape a humdrum (boring) life

Other possible important reasons why men volunteered are:

- posters showed men that women wanted them to join the war
- posters encouraged men to join for 'Poor Little Belgium'
- posters encouraged men to join so as not to be disgraced
- many joined because of the adventure
- some joined hoping for glory and medals
- some joined to gain meaningful employment and better pay
- some joined to avoid accusations of being a coward or being given a white feather
- some joined to be with friends in 'Pals Battalions'

2.

See page 14 for more help. | KU2 (out of 4 marks). Remember that to get full marks you must have at least one piece of remembered information in your answer.

Evidence from the source to explain why German civilians were experiencing difficulties by 1918 is:

- Britain blockaded German ports and caused hunger
- millions of men were fighting so there was less men working on fields, so many Germans starved
- supplies ran short

Other possible evidence to explain why German civilians experienced difficulties includes:

- anti-Kaiser riots had started in large German towns by 1918
- anti-war protests started in some towns
- bread riots began to break out as supplies ran short
- Communist uprisings started in some towns
- influenza spread, killing many malnourished civilians
- the British naval blockage also meant vital supplies such as medicines and fuel did not get through

3.

See page 28 for more help. ES4 (out of 3 marks). Remember that to get full marks, you must have at least one piece of evidence from the source and at least one piece of evidence from remembered information in your answer.

The **evidence from the source** about naval rivalry between Britain and Germany is:

- Britain launched the HMS *Dreadnought*
- Germany built a 'Dreadnought' as well
- there was a competition for the most number of large ships
- by 1914 Britain was winning the competition: 29–17

Other possible evidence about naval rivalry includes:

- HMS *Dreadnought* was better armed/faster than other warships
- HMS *Dreadnought* made all other ships obsolete
- Britain built new naval bases (at Scapa and Rosyth)
- Germany built new naval bases
- Germany widened the Kiel Canal to take bigger battleships
- building more ships became a national obsession

4.

See page 19 for more help. ES1 (out of 4 marks). Remember to state whether the source is useful or of limited use.

Source D is useful as evidence of the problems in the Balkans before World War One because:

- it is a primary source written at the time (of troubles in the Balkans) {contemporaneity}
- it was written by the compilers of the Black Hand Constitution {authorship}
- it gives good information about the aims of the Black Hand in the Balkans {content}
- it is a true account, matching your own knowledge **which you must give** {accuracy}
- it was written to set out the aims of the Black Hand in the Balkans {purpose}
- however, it is a biased commentary on the situation {limitation}

5.

See page 23 for more help. ES2 (out of 4 marks). Remember that you get one mark for a simple comparison (marked*) and two marks for a developed comparison.

Here are some of the ways in which the sources agree:

*The Sources agree that the Black Hand was a secret society:

Source D says: is an absolutely secret one

Source E says: Black Hand Secret Society

*The Sources agree that the aim of the Black Hand was to unite all Serbs:

Source D says: the purpose of Unification of all Serbs

Source E says: to unite all Serb people

*The Sources agree that an aim was to create a bigger/more powerful Serbia:

Source D says: in an enlarged state of Serbia

Source E says: unite in a 'Greater Serbia'

*The Sources agree that the Black Hand aimed to use violence to achieve its end:

Source D says: fight with all means

Source E says: by means of violence

*The Sources agree that the society was fanatical:

Source D says: revolutionary organisation

Source E says: used terrorist action

*The Sources agree that its badge/seal included the death head (skull) symbol:

Source D shows: death's head/head of a human skeleton

Source E says: badge with its death head symbol

Unit III, Context D

1.

See page 14 for more help. KU2 (out of 3 marks). Remember that to get full marks you must have at least one piece of remembered information in your answer.

Evidence from the source explaining why German people faced difficulties during the hyperinflation crisis is:

• food prices went up
• a kilo of bread cost 163 marks in January 1923 and 9 million marks by October 1923

Other possible evidence explaining why German people faced difficulties includes:

- money became worthless very quickly
- many resorted to bartering for goods rather than using money
- people had to collect wages in suitcases
- petty crime increased
- the black market prospered
- people who had loaned to others were paid back but the money was worthless
- those with savings were ruined as savings were now worth nothing
- some people lost their jobs

2.

See page 11 for more help. KU1 (out of 4 marks). Remember that to get full marks you must have at least one piece of remembered information in your answer.

Evidence from the source describing the methods used by Hitler to make the Jews inferior is:

- Jewish shops were boycotted
- the Star of David was painted on German Jews' shop windows
- German Jews' shops had placards put up on them or were daubed

Other possible evidence describing the methods used by Hitler to make the Jews inferior includes:

- Jewish synagogues and houses were damaged and destroyed in the Night of the Broken Glass (Kristallnacht)
- German Jews had to wear the Star of David
- German Jews passports were stamped with a 'J'
- German Jews were forced out of housing
- German Jews were forced out of Civil Service Jobs
- Nuremburg Laws, which persecuted Jews, were passed
- German Jews could not marry non-Jewish Germans
- Jews were banned from public parks and swimming pools

3.

See page 26 for more help. ES3 (out of 3 marks). Remember to discuss the author's attitude to the event or issue.

The attitude of the author about the 1933 election is that he:

- was not happy at the way it was carried out
- was complaining that it was unfair
- hated the way people were made to vote for Hitler
- accused Hitler/ the Nazis of rigging the election
- believed people were forced (at gunpoint) to vote for Hitler

4.

See page 23 for more help. ES2 (out of 4 marks). Remember that you get one mark for a simple comparison (marked*) and two marks for a developed comparison.

Here are some of the ways in which the sources agree:

*The Sources agree that the election was not fair/democratic:

Source C shows: unfair methods of making someone vote

Source D says: hardly a fair/democratic one

*The Sources agree that Hitler/Nazis used unreasonable/violent tactics:

Source C shows: Hitler brandishing gun and dagger

Source D says: Hitler took strong action to ensure the result/

Nazis used bullying methods

*The Sources agree that the Nazis 'managed' the vote:

Source C shows: leader of the Nazis using force

Source D says: Nazis controlled the voting process

However:

*Only Source D says the election came after the Reichstag Fire

*Only Source D says that the Reichstag Fire gave Hitler/Nazis more power

Answers   **General Paper C**

Unit I, Context B

1.

See page 11 for more help. | KU1 (out of 3 marks). Remember that to get full marks you must have at least one piece of remembered information in your answer.

Evidence from the source describing housing conditions in Scottish towns is:

- houses were cramped together with little room between them
- houses were poorly built and could collapse

Other possible evidence describing housing conditions includes:

- overcrowding in housing was a major problem
- houses had poor sanitation with no indoor toilets
- many people had to share one outdoor toilet (a privy)
- there were no separate rooms
- many people from one family lived in one/two rooms- overcrowding caused diseases to spread
- there was poor ventilation
- many houses were damp
- many houses were often subdivided time and time again and this weakened housing structures

2.

See page 14 for more help. | KU2 (out of 4 marks). Remember that to get full marks you must have at least one piece of remembered information in your answer.

Evidence from the source explaining why working conditions had improved for farm workers is:

- Bell's reaper did the work of many more men and animals
- steam threshing machines did the work far quicker

Other possible evidence explaining why working conditions improved includes:

- tractors did the work of many men
- machines were used to sow seeds such as the Tull Drill (invented in 1700s but not used extensively until much later)
- machines were used to weed fields
- machines were used to spread fertilisers
- machines were used to reap and bind crops
- combine harvesters began to be used
- new ploughs made work much quicker and easier
- introduction of steam power made processing crops quicker and cheaper

3.

See page 19 for more help. ES1 (out of 3 marks). Remember to state whether the source is useful or of limited use.

Source C is useful as evidence of the causes of population growth in Scotland between 1850 and 1914 because:

- it is a secondary source written with the benefit of hindsight {contemporaneity}
- it was written by a professional historian who has researched the topic {authorship}
- it gives good information about population growth (with an example) {content}
- it is a factual account, matching your own (**and given**) knowledge {accuracy}
- it was written to inform the readers of historical development {purpose}
- however, it is only one viewpoint/ opinion {limitation}

4.

See page 30 for more help. ES5 (out of 5 marks). A maximum of three marks can be awarded if the relevant evidence is selected for only one side of the issue.

Evidence for the issue, from Source C:

- mothers becoming better nourished
- well fed babies lived/ fewer babies died of hunger
- cheaper food prices helped to feed people
- more foodstuff from overseas helped

Evidence against the issue, from Source D:

- immigration affected the population
- living standards improved
- environmental conditions improved

5.

See page 30 for more help. ES6 (out of 5 marks). A conclusion which takes account of one side only and/or is based solely on either presented evidence or recall can be awarded a maximum of two marks.

A good, balanced conclusion is reached using **presented evidence** such as that listed above, and also **at least one point of recalled information such as:**

For the issue:

- agricultural revolution helped to feed urban population
- better farming methods/enclosure movement increased food production
- the quality of food improved
- urban working class could eat grain, milk, potatoes and meat from Scottish farms
- transport of food into towns improved
- mothers became more fertile – had more babies

Against the issue:

- earlier marriages produced more babies
- there was a lack of effective contraception
- there were improvements in hygiene/soap and public water supplies

- a better water supply in towns helped reduce deaths
- better sewerage in towns reduced disease
- vaccination against smallpox reduced deaths
- an improvement in clothing brought better hygiene
- improving medical knowledge saved lives
- there was immigration from Ireland and areas of Europe

Unit II, Context A

1.

See page 15 for more help. KU3 (out of 3 marks). Remember that to get full marks you must have at least one piece of remembered information in your answer.

Evidence from the source about the importance of artillery in World War One is:

- all hours of the day, artillery fired on soldiers
- artillerymen were quite accurate
- soldiers were scared by the sound of shells passing and exploding

Other possible evidence about the importance of artillery includes:

- artillery attacks kept the enemy hidden in dugouts
- soldiers suffered from shell shock after heavy and prolonged bombardments
- for protection some soldiers had to hide in dugouts
- German dugouts in particular were well built and could withstand heavy artillery bombardments
- artillery bombardments could give the enemy forewarning of a coming attack
- mention may be made of other weapons that were important also: e.g. machine guns, gas, grenades, and tanks

2.

See page 11 for more help. KU1 (out of 4 marks). Remember that to get full marks you must have at least one piece of remembered information in your answer.

Evidence from the source describing the land terms of the Treaty of Versailles is:

- there were minor adjustments to the German border with Belgium.
- Alsace and Lorraine were returned to France
- Saarland coalfields to be exploited by France

Other possible evidence about the land terms of the treaty includes:

- the left bank of the Rhine, the Rhineland, was to be a demilitarised zone
- North Schleswig was to be given to Denmark
- Danzig became a free city/port to be administered by the League of Nations
- Polish Corridor was given to Poland
- Upper Silesia was to be given to Poland
- German unification with Austria (Anschluss) was forbidden
- East Prussia was separated from the rest of Germany by the Polish corridor
- minor adjustments were made to the frontier with Belgium/ Belgium was to gain some land
- Germany was banned from uniting with Austria (Anschluss) in the future

3.

> *See page 19 for more help.* ES1 (out of 3 marks). Remember to state whether the source is useful or of limited use.

Source C is useful as evidence of conditions in Germany towards the end of World War One because:

- it is a primary source taken at the time (in 1918/towards the end of World War One) {contemporaneity}
- it was taken by an eyewitness cameraman {authorship}
- it gives good details of the conditions in Germany in 1918 (with an example) {content}
- it is a photograph showing information matching your own (**and given**) knowledge {accuracy}
- it was taken to record events in Germany at the time {purpose}
- however, it is only one photograph/ it needs more evidence {limitation}

4.

> *See page 23 for more help.* ES2 (out of 4 marks). Remember that you get one mark for a simple comparison (marked *) and two marks for a developed comparison.

Here are some of the ways in which the sources agree:

*The Sources agree that by 1918 the war was getting serious for German civilians:

Source C says/shows: people in Germany suffering/ having to barter for wood

Source D says: the longer the war lasted, the more serious it became

*The Sources agree that people ate (lots of) potatoes:

Source C says/shows: women with bags of potato peelings

Source D says: lived on a diet of potatoes

*The Sources agree that people (farmers) collected household food waste:

Source C says/shows: people (farmers) collecting potato peelings

Source D says: farmers collected food waste

*The Sources agree that by 1918 there was a shortage of fuel:

Source C shows/says: women exchanging potato peelings for firewood

Source D says: in early 1918 there was a fuel shortage

*The Sources agree that mothers would do anything to keep their children warm:

Source C says/shows: mothers exchanging possible food for fuel

Source D says: mothers would go to any length to keep children warm

However:

*Only Source D says that people were nearly starving

*Only Source D says that people ate sawdusty bread

*Only Source D says that people were dying of cold

Unit III, Context D

1.

See page 15 for more help. KU3 (out of 4 marks). Remember that to get full marks you must have at least one piece of remembered information in your answer.

Evidence from the source about the importance of the Beer Hall Putsch in the Nazis' rise to power is:

- the march was not successful as it was brought to a halt by police gunfire
- Hitler was arrested and imprisoned
- Hitler gained respect from the army as he had Ludendorff by his side

Other possible evidence about the importance of the Beer Hall Putsch includes:

- a number of Hitler's men were killed or injured on the day of the Putsch
- Hitler used the trial to give anti-government speech
- the trial got Hitler a lot of publicity
- Hitler was jailed for nine months and not the longer sentence he deserved (this showed the judges sympathised with him)

there were other factors which helped Hitler rise to power such as:

- the Wall Street Crash
- the weaknesses of Weimar Republic
- the Reichstag Fire
- the Enabling Act
- the Night of the Long Knives

2.

See page 11 for more help. KU1 (out of 3 marks). Remember that to get full marks you must have at least one piece of remembered information in your answer.

Evidence from the source describing some of the methods used to persecute Jewish people in Germany is:

- Jewish synagogues were burned down as part of Kristallnacht
- Jewish synagogues had their windows smashed

Other possible evidence describing some of the methods used to persecute the Jewish people includes:

- Jewish shops were boycotted
- Germans who bought from German Jews were added to the (Pranger) List which was displayed publicly
- German Jews had to wear the Star of David
- German Jews' passports were stamped with a 'J'
- German Jews were forced out of housing
- German Jews were forced out of Civil Service Jobs
- Nuremburg Laws, which persecuted Jews, were passed
- German Jews could not marry non-Jewish Germans
- Jews were banned from public parks and swimming pools

3.

See page 28 for more help. ES4 (out of 3 marks). Remember that to get full marks, you must have at least one piece of evidence from the source and at least one piece of evidence from remembered information in your answer.

The **evidence given in Source C** about why the Weimar Republic collapsed is:

- National Socialism offered a more successful solution
- the failure of Weimar to solve 1929 financial collapse
- the Nazis launched a large scale propaganda campaign
- the Nazis promised a social revolution
- German youth wanted a restoration of order

Other possible evidence why the Weimar republic collapsed includes:

- Weimar was blamed for losing World War One
- Weimar was associated with the hated Treaty of Versailles
- it was blamed for the burden of reparations
- it seemed unable to control outbreaks of violence
- it was criticised for weak coalition governments / weak leadership
- it was criticised by nationalists for giving in to foreign powers
- it was criticised for French invasion of Ruhr
- it was blamed for rising unemployment
- there was a desire for strong rule/ dictatorship
- (you could give further evidence on the appeal of the Nazis)

4.

See page 23 for more help. ES2 (out of 4 marks). Remember that you get one mark for a simple comparison (marked*) and two marks for a developed comparison.

Here are some of the ways in which the sources agree:

*The Sources agree that the Nazis promised a better government:

Source D says: National Socialism offered a more successful solution

Source E says: National Socialism offered a promise of better things

*The Sources agree that the Nazis took advantage of the financial collapse:

Source D says: Nazi party took advantage of economic depression

Source E says: Nazis seemed to offer a solution to the suffering of economic depression

*The Sources agree that the Nazis seemed to offer more order in the country:

Source D says: Germans longed for the restoration of ordered existence

Source E says: Nazis offered a picture of order

*The Sources agree that the Nazis had an effective advertising campaign:

Source D says: Nazis launched a large scale propaganda machine which won mass following

Source E says: Nazi newspapers/rallies offered a more stable government

However:

Only Source D says the Nazis appealed to young people

Only Source E says people were attracted to Nazi troopers in smart uniforms

5.

See page 26 for more help. ES3 (out of 3 marks). Remember to discuss the author's attitude to the event or issue.

The attitude of the author towards the Reichstag Fire is that he:

- was astonished at the blaze
- does not believe it was caused by the Communists
- believes it was caused by the Nazis
- thinks Hitler is using it as an excuse

Answers   **Credit Paper A**

Unit I, Context B

1.

> *See page 14 for more help.*   KU2 (out of 3 marks). Remember to use your points to actually explain the historical event or issue.

The impact of Irish immigrants on Scotland was that:

- they filled jobs
- the jobs they took were initially manual in nature (e.g. railway navvies, canal navvies, factory workers)
- many Scots resented the Irish taking 'their' jobs
- many of the Irish immigrants were Roman Catholic and they brought their religion with them
- some immigrants were Protestant and some participated in Orange Order activities
- religious rivalries were rife especially in the west of Scotland
- Irish immigrants had fun made out of them in political cartoons and newspapers
- immigrants tended to settle in major cities in the first instance (e.g. Glasgow, Edinburgh, Dundee)
- Catholic Irish set up social clubs, church clubs, charities and even football teams (e.g. Celtic FC, Hibernian FC, and Dundee Hibernian)

2.

> *See page 15 for more help.*   KU3 (out of 4 marks). Remember to explain how important any factor is, in comparison to other factors.

The importance of the 1842 Coal Mines Act was that:

- it banned women from working underground
- it banned children under the age of ten from working underground
- it enacted that women and children could still work above the surface in sorting and bagging coal
- it appointed inspectors to enforce it
- women dressed as men and hid long hair or cut it in order to continue working
- many underaged boys continued to work

But also:

- the number of inspectors was not enough to adequately enforce the Act
- further Government Acts had to be passed in 1850, 1860, and 1872
- the improvements these acts brought

New technology also improved mine safety such as:

- steam pumps and ventilation systems
- the Davy Safety lamp
- the use of animals and later machines for pulling heavy and dangerous loads
- pit props were made better when iron and steel replaced wood

3.

> *See page 19 for more help.* ES1 (out of 4 marks). Remember to state whether the source is useful or of limited use.

Source A is useful for investigating the Suffragette movement in the period 1903 to 1914 because:

- it is a primary source written at the time of the Suffragette movement {contemporaneity}
- it was written by an involved participant; the leader of the Suffragette movement {authorship}
- it gives good details of the Suffragette cause/Suffragette actions (give an example) {content}
- it's a factual account, matching your own (**and given**) knowledge {accuracy}
- it was written to communicate information/feelings to a fellow Suffragette {purpose}
- however, it's a biased commentary from a Suffragette activist {limitation}

4.

> *See page 30 for more help.* ES5 (out of 6 marks). A maximum of three marks can be awarded if the relevant evidence is selected for only one side of the issue.

Evidence selected and organised for the issue:

Source A:
- no commitment from government that they will give votes to women
- must continue to show determination
- women have been disappointed in the past
- it is a just cause/ worth fighting for

Source B:
- Government is torturing women
- Government is driving/forcing women into rebellion
- Government is force feeding Suffragettes

Source C:
- some sympathy with the Suffragette cause

Evidence selected and organised against the issue:

Source A:
- Suffragettes are not giving up – even when Parliament is discussing the issue
- Suffragettes are causing public disorder

Source B:
- Suffragettes are causing outrage/ outrageous acts
- Suffragettes have burned down a beautiful, medieval church

Source C:
- Suffragettes are committing illegal actions
- militancy is a disgrace
- militancy is hindering Votes for Women cause
- women should use constitutional means to get the vote

5.

See page 30 for more help. ES6 (out of 5 marks). A conclusion which takes account of one side only and/or is based solely on presented evidence or recalled information can be awarded a maximum of two marks.

A good, balanced conclusion is reached using **presented evidence** such as that listed above, and at least one point of **recalled information such as:**

For the issue:

- militant actions showed determination
- forceful actions gained the militant Suffragettes a lot of publicity
- forceful actions gained a great deal of public sympathy
- militancy caused the government great embarrassment
- militant actions annoyed insurance companies who put pressure on government
- women being treated like common criminals and sent to jail won sympathy
- martyrdom of Emily Davison won support

Against the issue:

- militant acts damaged property/MPs' houses etc.
- militancy often targeted male areas of interest, e.g. golf courses
- militant acts put many people/ the press off
- government had to show they will not give in to people who break the law
- encouraged other groups to break the law to try and get what they wanted
- highlighted how foolish and irresponsible women were being / too silly to be trusted with vote
- government had other urgent priorities to deal with

Unit II, Context A

1a.

See page 15 for more help. KU3 (out of 8 marks). Remember to explain how important any factor is, in comparison to other factors.

The importance of imperial rivalries as a cause of World War One is that:

- Britain wanted to retain the largest empire in the world
- Germany was ambitious and was building her empire
- the Kaiser was especially jealous of the British Empire
- the Kaiser wanted Germany to have her 'place in the sun'
- the 'Scramble for Africa' involved all European powers and increased tension

Possible reference to the other reasons given below in **1b.**

1b. The importance of nationalism in the Balkans as a cause of World War One is that:

- the collapse of the Turkish Empire left a power vacuum which Austria Hungary was eager to fill
- small countries being taken over by Austria Hungary were extremely nationalist and resisted
- Austria Hungary and Russia were rivals in the Balkans
- Russia supported the Slavs (and wanted a warm water port)

- there had been Balkan Wars in the area before the outbreak of World War One
- Gavrilo Princip assassinated the archduke to the Austria Hungarian throne, Franz Ferdinand
- Austria Hungary blamed the Serbian Black Hand gang
- Austria Hungary issued an ultimatum to Serbia following the assassinations
- Serbia did not accept all the points in the ultimatum
- Austria Hungary declared war on Serbia
- this sparked a chain of events involving the alliance system that led to World War One

And possible reference to:

- Russia mobilised in support of Serbia
- Germany issued Austria Hungary a 'blank cheque'
- Alliance system (Triple Alliance and Triple Entente) had a part to play
- there had been an arms race in Europe leading up to the war
- there had been economic rivalries between the Great Powers

And also possible reference to the factors given in **1a.**

2.

> See page 26 for more help. ES3 (out of 3 marks). Remember to discuss the author's attitude to the event or issue.

The attitude of the author towards trench conditions is that he:

- disliked them
- hated the mud/ wet
- put up with the discomfort
- made fun/ironic jokes about the conditions
- hated winters more

3.

> See page 23 for more help. ES2 (out of 5 marks). Remember that you get one mark for a simple comparison (marked*) and two marks for a developed comparison.

Here are some of the ways in which the sources agree:

*The Sources agree that the trenches were muddy:

Source A shows: soldiers in the mud

Source B says: nothing but mud

*The Sources agree that the trenches were filthy/dirty/a mess:

Source A shows: debris/ messy conditions

Source B says: nothing but filth

*The Sources agree that soldiers became dirty/unkempt

Source A shows: dirty soldiers

Source B says: looked like tramps/plastered with filth and dirt

*The Sources agree that soldiers' clothes got wet/dirty/muddy:

Source A shows: muddy coats

Source B says: overcoats were sodden/muddy/wet

*The Sources agree that it was hard to keep rifle/bayonet clean:

Source A shows: rifle/bayonet in the mud

Source B says: impossible to keep Lee Enfield rifle/ bayonet clean

4.

See page 28 for more help. ES4 (out of 5 marks). Remember that to get full marks, you must have at least one piece of evidence from the source and at least one piece of evidence from remembered information in your answer.

The **evidence given in Source C** about a gas attack is:

- gas came over in a green cloud
- one type of gas was chlorine
- early attempts to counteract gas used urine-soaked cloth
- poison gas attacked the lungs
- enemy soldiers attacked after the gas

Other possible evidence about a gas attack is:

- gas was released from canisters or (later) shells
- gases included phosgene/ mustard gas
- gas burned eyes and skin
- later gas masks were more effective
- gas could change direction and affect the attackers

Unit III, Context D

1.

See page 11 for more help. KU1 (out of 3 marks). To gain full marks, you must use your own knowledge.

The failings of the Weimar Republic are:

- it was blamed for losing World War One
- conservatives, nationalists and disgruntled army officers created the 'stab in the back' theory against it
- it was associated with signing the hated Treaty of Versailles
- the voting system of proportional representation created weak/coalition governments and disillusionment with the democratic system
- it had a series of weak and ineffective leaders
- proportional representation allowed small extremist parties to gain seats and a voice in the Reichstag
- it suffered from attacks from the Left (Spartacist Revolt) and the Right (Kapp Putsch and Munich Putsch)

- it appeared unable to stop rioting, political assassinations and the breakdown of law and order
- Article 48 gave emergency powers to the president and was misused
- in 1923 it was blamed for the economic crisis (following the failure to pay reparations)
- it was criticised for the French/Belgian invasion of the Ruhr (in 1923)
- it was blamed for the hyperinflation that ensued and left many jobless
- it was blamed for the effects of 1929 Wall Street Crash
- it never inspired confidence of people who desired a return to strong leadership/ dictatorship

2.

> See page 14 for more help.
> KU2 (out of 4 marks). Remember to use your points to actually explain the historical event or issue.

The Nazis used the Reichstag Fire as follows:

- Hitler used it as publicity stunt
- Hitler blamed the communists for the fire
- Hitler used van der Lubbe as a scapegoat
- Hitler convinced Hindenburg to issue him with emergency powers
- Nazis arrested thousands of communists after the fire
- Nazis used the fire to remove civil liberties and began tapping phones lines/ intercepting mail
- Hitler passed the Enabling Act which gave him complete power in the Reichstag
- democracy ended as the Nazis set up a one party state
- Trade Unions were banned
- Nazis were placed into local government roles

3.

> See page 19 for more help.
> ES1 (out of 4 marks). Remember to state whether the source is useful or of limited use.

Source A is useful as evidence of the appeal of Nazi youth groups because:

- it is a primary source created at the time of Nazi youth movements {contemporaneity}
- it was drawn by a German poster artist, working for the Nazis {authorship}
- it gives good details of Nazi boys' youth movement (select an example) {content}
- it gives good factual content, matching your own (**and given**) knowledge {accuracy}
- it was created to persuade boys to join the Nazi youth movement {purpose}
- however, it is a biased portrayal/ from a Nazi perspective {limitation}

4.

See page 23 for more help. ES2 (out of 5 marks). Remember that you get one mark for a simple comparison (marked*) and two marks for a developed comparison.

Here are some of the ways in which the sources agree:

*The Sources agree that a Nazi youth movement resembled the Boy Scouts:

Source A shows: boy in uniform/neckerchief/shorts

Source B says: like a version of Boy Scouts

*The Sources agree that Nazi Youth wore uniforms:

Source A shows: boy in uniform

Source B says: uniformed team work

*The Sources agree that there was a military agenda:

Source A shows: a German soldier marching alongside the boy

Source B says: military agenda

*The Sources agree that youth movements were a preparation for the army:

Source A shows/says: boy pleased to be a future soldier/officer of tomorrow

Source B says: preparation for the army

However:

*Only Source B mentions team work

*Only Source B mentions training in marksmanship/weaponry/ boxing

Answers **Credit Paper B**

Unit I, Context B

1.

See page 11 for more help. KU1 (out of 4 marks). To gain full marks, you must use your own knowledge.

The impact of Scottish emigrants was that:

- they filled jobs in a variety of countries
- many took on land and were successful in farming
- many were happier with the new living conditions
- many were happy to have jobs / land / a house which they did not have in Scotland (or had better ones abroad than they had in Scotland)
- some did not find jobs / land / a house very easily
- they set kept their Scottish roots and kept Scottish culture alive wherever they went
- many had to work in hard manual jobs upon arrival and were not well paid
- many had to live in expensive rented accommodation on arrival in new countries

2.

See page 14 for more help. KU2 (out of 3 marks). Remember to use your points to actually explain the historical event or issue.

The difficulties in building railways was that:

- land had to be flat
- tunnels had to be dug through mountains
- tunnelling was hard work and was done by hand, until the introduction of explosive charges
- at Olive Mount a cutting two miles long had to be made in the rock
- valleys had to be filled with viaducts
- marshland had to be shored up
- following the Gauge Act (1846) all railways had be built with the same gauge
- viaducts and bridges were expensive to build and took time
- cheap labour had to be found to build railways
- navvies who built railways often brought violence and drunkenness to areas they worked in

3.

See page 19 for more help. ES1 (out of 4 marks). Remember to state whether the source is useful or of limited use.

Source A is useful for investigating housing in Scotland in the late nineteenth and early twentieth centuries because:

- it is a primary source written at the time of early twentieth century housing conditions {contemporaneity}
- it is an official report/ government census document {authorship}
- it gives good details of housing conditions in Scotland (give an example) {content}

- it is a factual account, matching your own (**and given**) knowledge {accuracy}
- it was written to record information about Scotland's people {purpose}
- however, it is limited statistical information/ requires additional evidence {limitation}

4.

See page 30 for more help. ES5 (out of 6 marks). A maximum of three marks can be awarded if the relevant evidence is selected for only one side of the issue.

Evidence selected and organised for the issue:

Source A:
- very few homes with no windows
- number of one roomed homes has dropped
- housing conditions better in small burghs

Source B:
- some improvement by 1880
- better off ploughman's cottages (by 1880s)

Source C:
- Housing Acts improved conditions
- Government helped local authorities build council houses
- private house building was encouraged
- people bought houses with proper amenities

Evidence selected and organised against the issue:

Source A:
- high number live in two roomed houses
- half of all Scots live two or more to a room
- Scottish overcrowding worse than in England
- many homes in Glasgow share a toilet

Source B:
- very low door/walls
- poor materials: turf, rough stones
- floor is bare earth

Source C:
- still far from well-housed (by 1930s)
- overcrowding still existed (in 1930s)
- city slums existed (in 1930s)
- inadequate bothies still existed (in 1930s)

5.

See page 30 for more help. ES6 (out of 5 marks). A conclusion which takes account of one side only and/or is based solely on presented evidence or recalled information can be awarded a maximum of two marks.

A good, balanced conclusion is reached using **presented evidence** such as that listed above, and also **at least one piece of recalled information such as:**

For the issue:

- Artisans and Labourers Dwelling Act (1875)/large-scale clearance programmes

- new houses were substantial/ made of good materials
- houses were often built of stone and brick
- Addison Housing Act (1919)
- Chamberlain Housing Act (1923)
- Wheatley Housing Act (1924)
- Greenwood Housing Act (1930)

In the country:

- slate was replacing thatch roofs
- wooden or stone floors were laid
- glass was put in windows
- new dwellings had fireplaces and chimneys
- running water being installed
- flush toilets / septic tanks beginning to be installed
- kitchen equipment / ranges were also improving
- had other amenities such as barns etc for animals

Against the issue:

- relevant detail of inadequate housing still in existence
- colliers' houses still poor
- tenement slum conditions still existed
- cooking often still done on open fire
- some chimneys were still holes in the roof
- animals still shared accommodation in rural dwellings
- sanitation could still be primitive/non-existent
- poor ventilation still existed
- lighting was still inefficient

Unit II, Context A

1a.

> *See page 15 for more help.* KU3 (out of 8 marks). Rmember to explain how important any factor is, in comparison to other factors.

The importance of poor tactics used by commanders as a cause of allied casualties in World War One is that:

- many commanders only had experience in Napoleonic war tactics
- some commanders still held to cavalry-based tactics which were of little use in the trenches
- tactics were no use when used against modern technology (e.g. machine guns)
- many commanders were cavalry men/ not used to infantry warfare
- commanders used artillery to poor effect against strong German dug outs
- commanders made poor use of intelligence
- commanders did not capitalise on break through opportunities (e.g. the 36th Ulster Division's advance at the Somme)
- commanders used gas to ill effect early on (e.g. at Loos where it blew back into the attackers trenches)
- commanders told men to walk over in waves on the first day of the Somme, this made them easy targets
- commanders at the Somme insisted that soldiers took full kit with them: this weighed them down

- the timing of artillery attacks and infantry assaults often was poorly coordinated
- commanders did not alter plans in accordance with weather and other conditions (e.g. Passchendaele)

Possible reference to the factors are mentioned in **1b** below.

1b. The importance of disease in the trenches as a cause of allied casualties in World War One is that:

- soldiers suffered from trench foot when immersed in water for prolonged periods
- soldiers suffered from dysentery when exposed to insanitary conditions
- dead bodies contaminated the ground around soldiers
- rats fed off dead bodies and carried diseases
- soldiers' immune systems were low, given the poor, cold conditions they were living in
- there was a lack of clean drinking water, with water brought up in cans previously used to hold oil
- there were only basic treatments available for disease at front line field dressing stations
- many soldiers suffered from disease and gangrene following even minor wounds

And possible reference to the factors mentioned in **1a** above.

2.

See page 19 for more help. ES1 (out of 4 marks). Remember to state whether the source is useful or of limited use.

Source A is useful as evidence of life in Britain during World War One because:

- it is a secondary source written after the event but with benefit of hindsight {contemporaneity}
- it was written by a professional historian who has researched the subject {authorship}
- it gives good details of Zeppelin raids during World War One (give an example) {content}
- it is a factual account, matching your own (**and given**) knowledge {accuracy}
- it was written to inform readers of life during World War One {purpose}
- however, it is just one account; requires further corroboration {limitation}

3.

See page 26 for more help. ES3 (out of 3 marks). Remember to discuss the author's attitude to the event or issue.

The attitude of the author towards air raids is that she was:

- anxious/worried about the raids/ the suspense of the unknown
- not really frightened/ quite brave
- hoping it would not last long/ be over soon
- awe-struck/ captivated/very interested in the bombing

4.

See page 28 for more help. ES4 (out of 5 marks). Remember that to get full marks, you must have at least one piece of evidence from the source and at least one piece of evidence from remembered information in your answer.

The evidence given in **Sources A** and **B** about how the war affected the lives of British civilians is that:

- civilians were attacked by Zeppelins
- they were bombed
- they had to take cover during attacks
- they had to black out windows
- they were affected as in no other war
- they had the press censored by DORA
- they were still able to read about raids in the press

Other possible evidence about how the war affected the lives of British civilians such as:

- German Gotha planes attacked civilians
- air raids caused damage/casualties
- there were food shortages and rationing
- there was the existence of a black market
- there were the worries of having men away at war and the possibility of them being wounded/killed
- some women became nurses
- some women worked on the land
- there were other DORA restrictions
- the effects of propaganda
- the effects of conscription

Unit III, Context D

1.

See page 15 for more help. KU3 (out of 3 marks). Remember to explain how important any factor is, in comparison to other factors.

The importance of the Treaty of Versailles in causing problems for the Weimar Republic is that:

- the Weimar Republic was blamed for signing the hated treaty
- they were forced to sign War Guilt clause which led to poor moral
- the limits on the army made internal and external security difficult
- the limits on the navy and the ban on the air force caused difficulties in securing Germany's borders
- the land loss left many Germans in a country not of their birth
- the land loss left some German's in East Prussia, isolated from Germany
- the Reparations caused major economic difficulties: unemployment / hyperinflation

And other possible factors such as:

- the voting system of proportional representation created weak/coalition governments and disillusionment with democratic system
- PR allowed small extremist parties to gain seats and a voice in the Reichstag

- they had series of weak and ineffective leaders
- they suffered from attacks from the Left (Spartacist Revolt) and the Right (Kapp Putsch and Munich Putsch)
- they appeared unable to stop rioting, political assassinations and the breakdown of law and order
- Article 48 gave emergency powers to the president and was misused
- they were blamed for the 1923 economic crisis (following the failure to pay reparations)
- they were criticised for the French/Belgian invasion of the Ruhr (1923)
- they were blamed for the hyperinflation that ensued and left many jobless
- they were blamed for the effects of 1929 Wall Street Crash
- they never inspired the confidence of people who desired a return to strong leadership / dictatorship

2.

See page 14 for more help. KU2 (out of 4 marks). Remember to use your points to actually explain the historical event or issue.

Some of the ways in which Hitler gained power are:

- he was helped by the weaknesses of the Weimar Republic, such as their poor constitution/problems of Versailles Treaty / economic difficulties in 1923 & 1929
- he was seen as a saviour figure and so was popular
- he was asked to assume the Chancellor's position by Hindenburg
- he provided strong leadership figure that German people wanted
- he promised jobs / rip up Treaty of Versailles / defeat communist menace
- he used good propaganda
- he used fear tactics to intimidate opponents using Brownshirts (SA)
- he blamed the Reichstag Fire on communists to gain Reichstag Fire Law (emergency powers)
- he arrested political opponents so there was no opposition
- he banned trade union movements
- he banned opposition press and publicity
- he crushed internal opponents in the Night of the Long Knives.
- He gained complete power on the death of Hindenburg in 1934 when he merged role of president and chancellor to Fuhrer (leader).
- he ensured he had support of army by forcing oath of loyalty.
- He placed Nazis in local government positions.

3.

See page 26 for more help. ES3 (out of 3 marks). Remember to discuss the auther's attitude to the event or issue.

The attitude of the author towards education for girls is that he:

- believes a woman's place is in the family/in the home
- thinks that it is a woman's duty to have children
- believes women are the teachers of the young/ the builders of the future
- thinks that women should stay in their roles: motherhood/ family – not in working life
- thinks girls should dress correctly/appropriately

4.

> *See page 23 for more help.* ES2 (out of 5 marks). Remember that you get one mark for a simple comparison (marked*) and two marks for a developed comparison.

Some of the ways in which the sources agree are:

*The Sources agree that Nazis thought that girls should be educated for a role in family life:

Source A says: teach children that most suitable place for women is in the family

Source B shows: woman in a family role/ looking after a child

*The Sources agree that women should produce children:

Source A says: a woman's duty is (to have) children

Source B shows: a woman with a child

*The Sources agree that women serve their nation by having children:

Source A says: serve her people in the motherhood of the German nation

Source B says: "Support the National Effort. Mother and child."

*The Sources agree that women should stick to perceived female roles:

Source A says: motherhood is real task/ leave working to men

Source B shows: woman as mother, man working in the fields/ ploughing

*The Sources agree that girls should be taught to dress appropriately:

Source A says: girls must be taught to dress correctly for her role

Source B shows: girl/woman in simple dress/ suitable clothes for feeding a baby

However:

*Only Source A says that woman is the teacher of young people/builder of the future

Answers   Credit Paper C

Unit I, Context B

1a.

> *See page 15 for more help.*   KU3 (out of 8 marks). Remember to explain how important any factor is, in comparison to other factors.

The importance of Government action in improving safety in coal mines between 1830 and 1930 is that:

- the 1842 Mines act forbade children under ten and women from working underground
- the 1842 Act made fifteen the minimum age for operating winding gear
- the 1850 Coal Mine inspectors act gave powers to inspectors and required accidents to be reported to the government
- the 1860 Act made it illegal for boys under twelve to go underground
- the 1860 Act made it a requirement for pits to have two points of exit
- the 1872 Mines Act made it a requirement for pit owners to posses a safety certificate
- the 1909 Act introduced the eight hour day which cut working hours
- 1911 Laws made it a requirement for mines to provide miners with baths

Possible reference to the factors mentioned in **1b** below.

1b. The importance of new technology in improving safety in coal mines between 1830 and 1930 is that:

- the Davy safety lamp prevented death from gas poisoning or explosions by gas
- air pumps introduced such as that invented by John Bundle
- ventilations fans were introduced to provide better air quality
- flooding was prevented by steam powered pumps (such as that invented by Watt). Later, electric pumps were introduced.
- better electric lighting was in place by 1930
- electric coal cutting machines and conveyor belts made life easier
- wagonways and trains were better at moving coal underground
- safer metal and concrete pit props were introduced
- better steam and electrical power was used to raise wire rope cages

And possible reference to the factors mentioned in **1a** above.

2.

> *See page 19 for more help.*   ES1 (out of 4 marks). Remember to state whether the source is useful or of limited use.

Source A is useful for investigating emigration from Scotland between 1840 and 1930 because:

- it is a secondary source written after the event but with benefit of hindsight {contemporaneity}
- it was written by a professional historian who has researched the subject {authorship}
- it gives good details of emigration from Scotland (give an example) {content}
- it is a factual account, matching your own (**and given**) knowledge {accuracy}

- it was written to inform readers about emigration from Scotland and/ or the Highland Clearances {purpose}
- however, it is just one account; requires further corroboration {limitation}

3.

See page 30 for more help. ES5 (out of 6 marks). A maximum of three marks can be awarded if the relevant evidence is selected for only one side of the issue.

Evidence selected and organised for the issue:

Source A:
- change was brutal
- many were forced to emigrate
- direct eviction occurred

Source B:
- saw houses swept away
- people were driven out of the countryside (to migrate to Glasgow/Canada)
- people went to live in the Canadian wilderness
- emigrant passages were terrible: hunger/disease
- people were crying at eviction
- people were forced to emigrate/board a ship
- the experience was loathsome

Source C:
- economic decline in Scotland caused emigration
- not all succeeded in their new country

Evidence selected and organised against the issue:

Source A:
- in some areas moving was done with consideration/skill
- people found other activities
- life was tough in the Highlands (for people without property)
- there was density of population/overcrowding/too many people for the land to support
- standard of living was low

Source B:
- some treated emigration with boldness
- some looked for adventure

Source C:
- many (emigrants) thrived
- many Scots helped to make/shape N. America and Australasia

4.

See page 30 for more help. ES6 (out of 5 marks). A conclusion which takes account of one side only and/or is based solely on presented evidence or recall can be awarded a maximum of two marks.

A good, balanced conclusion is reached using **presented evidence** such as that listed above, and at least one point of **recalled information such as:**

For the issue:

- the Clearances involved the destruction/burning of houses

- attempts to provide alternative employment (e.g. fishing) often failed
- migrant ships lacked regulation
- there was a sense of clan loss/culture breakdown
- life in an industrial city could be hard
- farm land in Canada had to be broken in

Against the issue:

- many Scots emigrated because of the better living/working prospects
- many had family to welcome them/there were many other Scots overseas
- Scottish emigrants were welcomed by Canadians
- the kelp crisis after the Napoleonic Wars drove many away
- crofting life was hard even after 1886 reforms, emigration was better
- Potato Famine in Highlands and Islands in 1840s made it better to emigrate
- there was plenty of land available abroad

Unit II, Context A

1.

See page 11 for more help. | KU1 (out of 4 marks). To gain full marks, you must use your own knowledge.

The tension which existed between the Great Powers was that:

- Britain had the largest empire in the world and this made other countries jealous
- Germany had imperial ambitious and was building her empire. The Kaiser said, "Germany will have her place in the sun"
- Germany was competing with Britain over naval power
- A Naval Arms race followed the launch of HMS *Dreadnought* in 1906
- there was industrial competition between the Great Powers
- rivalry existed between France and Germany following the Franco Prussian War
- France was eager for revenge on Germany following the loss of Alsace Lorraine (in the above war)
- Russia was keen to get a warm water port in the Balkans area
- other countries were suspicious of Russia's desires in the Balkans
- Austria Hungary and Russia were competing in the Balkans
- the 'Scramble for Africa' involved all European powers

2.

See page 11 for more help. | KU1 (out of 4 marks). To gain full marks, you must use your own knowledge.

The successes of the League of Nations were that:

- it settled dispute between Sweden and Finland over ownership of the Aaland Islands (1921)
- it threatened economic sanctions to persuade Serbia to remove its troops in a dispute with Albania (1921)
- it settled a dispute between Italy and Greece (1923)
- it settled a dispute between Greece and Bulgaria (1925)
- it settled a dispute between Iraq and Turkey (1925–26)

- it settled a dispute between Poland and Lithuania (1927)
- it made positive steps in repatriating refugees
- it did good work in famine relief
- it accepted Germany as a member (1926)

However:

- it had the problem of not having a standing army
- it did not have founder member, America, as a member
- it was weakened in not having Russia as member
- it was initially seen as a 'winners club'/ Germany was initially excluded

3.

See page 28 for more help. ES4 (out of 4 marks). Remember that to get full marks, you must have at least one piece of evidence from the source and at least one piece of evidence from remembered information in your answer.

The **evidence given in Source A** about the role of the tank in World War One is:

- tanks were eventually used in coordination with artillery and aircraft
- tanks were used to clear a path for infantry
- tanks were used in the Allied advances of 1918
- 604 Allied tanks were used in a mass attack
- the war ended before tanks could be fully utilised

Other possible evidence about the role of the tank is:

- early tank successes were few
- the tank was not technologically developed enough to make huge impact
- tanks were seen only as troop support – not as battle-winning weapons
- tanks were slow and could be immobilised
- tanks were awful to handle
- tanks were used too soon at the Somme in 1916
- the Battle of Cambrai was an initial success but was not followed up
- the Battle of Amiens was more successful

4.

See page 26 for more help. ES3 (out of 3 marks). Remember to explain how important any factor is, in comparison to other factors.

The attitude of the author of **Source B** about the Treaty of Versailles is that:

- he thought it very harsh
- he understands (to an extent) why it was punitive
- he thinks Germans will be disappointed with it
- he thinks it condemns Germany unduly
- he believes the financial punishment is too severe/reduces Germany to economic bondage

5.

See page 23 for more help. ES2 (out of 5 marks). Remember that you get one mark for a simple comparison (marked*) and two marks for a developed comparison.

Some of the ways in which the sources agree and disagree about the treatment of Germany at Versailles are:

*The Sources agree that Germany should accept blame for the war:

Source B says: we understand the bitter feelings of the Entente

Source C says: Germans are responsible

*The Sources agree that Germany should be punished for invading Belgium:

Source B says: we condemned the invasion of Belgium

Source C says: rulers of Germany violated the neutrality of Belgium

*The Sources agree that Germany should be blamed for war crimes:

Source B says: condemned crimes against humanity e.g. poison gas

Source C says: first to use poison gas (inflicting) appalling suffering

*The Sources agree that Germany is guilty of attacking civilians:

Source B says: Zeppelin raids on innocent civilians

Source C says: bombing of towns (and) striking at women and children

*The Sources disagree about how severely Germany should be punished:

Source B says: peace conditions are so hard

Source C says: there must be harsh justice

*The Sources disagree about the economic punishment:

Source B says: financial burden is so heavy/ Germany is reduced to economic bondage

Source C says: Germany must undertake to make financial reparation to the very uttermost of her power

---

Unit III, Context D

1.

See page 14 for more help. KU2 (out of 3 marks). Remember to use your points to actually explain the historical event or issue.

Many Germans disliked the Weimar Government in the 1920s because:

- they blamed it for losing World War One/ signing the armistice
- conservatives, nationalists and disgruntled army officers said it had 'stabbed them in the back'
- it was associated with signing the Treaty of Versailles
- Voting system of proportional representation created weak/coalition governments and disillusionment with democratic system
- it had a series of weak and ineffective leaders

- its system of proportional representation allowed small extremist parties to gain seats and a voice in the Reichstag
- it suffered from attacks from the Left (Spartacist Revolt) and the Right (Kapp Putsch and Munich Putsch)
- it appeared unable to stop rioting, political assassinations and the breakdown of law and order
- Article 48 gave emergency powers to the president and was misused
- it was blamed for the economic crisis following its failure to pay reparations
- it was criticised for the French/Belgian invasion of the Ruhr (1923)
- it was blamed for hyperinflation that ensued left many jobless
- it was blamed for the effects of the 1929 Wall Street Crash
- it never inspired confidence of people who desired return to strong leadership/dictatorship

2.

See page 11 for more help. | KU1 (out of 4 marks). To gain full marks, you must use your own knowledge.

Some attempts at opposing the Nazis came from:

- religious individuals who opposed the Nazis
- Martin Niemoller and Dietrich Bonhoffer who formed the Pastors Emergency League and issued papers against Nazis religious policies
- socialist, communist (KPD) and trade union opposition (limited and difficult as the leaders were arrested and newspapers and TUs were banned)
- cultural opposition to the Nazis by refusing to conform by dress, hair styles etc…
- limited open resistance (made difficult given the effectiveness of Nazi policing)
- some private grumbling
- some passive resistance

3.

See page 19 for more help. | ES1 (out of 4 marks). Remember to state whether the source is useful or of limited use.

Source A is useful as evidence of Nazi attitudes towards Jewish people because:

- it is a primary source written at the time of anti-Semitism in Germany {contemporaneity}
- it was written by Nazi official(s) compiling a book for Nazi Youth {authorship}
- it gives good details of anti-Jewish sentiment (give an example) {content}
- it is an accurate account, reflecting attitudes at the time; matched by your own **(and given)** knowledge {accuracy}
- it was written to fill young people with anti-Jewish ideas {purpose}
- however, it is a biased, Nazi, racist viewpoint {limitation}

4.

See page 28 for more help.

> ES4 (out of 4 marks). Remember that to get full marks, you must have at least one piece of evidence from the source and at least one piece of evidence from remembered information in your answer.

The evidence given in **Sources A** and **B** is that the aims of the Nazi Party were:

* to increase anti-Semitism/ hatred of Jewish people
* to remove Jewish people from German life
* a belief in an Aryan super race (Herrenvolk)
* a desire for Lebensraum (more living space for Germans)
* to conquer eastern Europe
* to fight against Bolshevism/ communism
* to oppose those who had betrayed Germany in 1918 (November Criminals)

Other possible evidence about the aims of the Nazi party such as:

* to get the Treaty of Versailles cancelled
* to restore the land lost in 1919
* to restore German pride
* to destroy democracy/ the Weimar Republic
* to pass laws against Jewish people, e.g. to remove them from the civil service
* to remove German citizenship from Jewish people
* to make Jewish people apart from other Germans: Nuremberg Laws
* to create a cult of the Fuhrer (Fuhrerprincip)

Acknowledgements

Leckie & Leckie is grateful to the copyright holders, as credited, for permission to use their material:

- Douglas MacKenzie; an extract from www.theclearances.org (page 20)
- Professor Gerhard Rempel; an extract from *The Nazi Road to Power* (page 28)
- Solo Syndication; a cartoon from the *London Evening Standard* (page 34)
- Imperial War Museum; a photograph (page 64)

The following people and organizations have very generously given permission to reproduce their material free of charge:

- Simon & Schuster UK Ltd; an extract from *The First World War* by Hew Strachan (page 22)
- Random House Group Ltd; three extracts from *Forgotten Voices from the Great War* by Max Arthur (pages 26 and 74) and an extract from *The Story of Britain* by Roy Strong (page 50)
- National Archives of Scotland; an extract from *Railway Records* (page 41)
- University of East Anglia; an extract from a letter written by Captain L Spicer from *PGCE History* (page 44)
- Penguin Books Ltd; two extracts from *The coming of the Third Reich* by Richard J Evans (pages 45 and 55); an extract from *The First World War* by AJP Taylor (page 53); an extract from *The Scottish Nation, 1750-2000* by Tom Devine (page 61)
- Routledge; an extract from *Nazi Germany Sourcebook* (quoting *Dachauer Tageblatt*) by Roderick Stackelberg and Sally Anne Winkle (page 46)
- History Learning Site; an extract from www.historylearningsite.com (page 46)
- An extract on page 53 from *Voices from War: Personal Recollections* of war in our century by Scottish men and women by Ian MacDougall is reproduced by permission of Mercat Press, an imprint of Birlinn Ltd (www.birlinn.co.uk)
- An extract on page 60 from *Scotland and Britain Since 1830* by Larry Cheyne and Sandra Chalmers is reproduced by permission of Edward Arnold (publishers) Ltd
- The Shetland Times Ltd; an extract from *Doing His Bit: A Shetland Soldier in the Great War* by Robert M Greig (page 62)
- Arcturus Publishing Limited; an extract from *Hitler: Military Commander* by Rupert Matthews (page 64)
- Federal Research Division of the Library of Congress; an extract from *Weimar Germany and the Rise of the Nazis* by Stephen Burant (page 65)
- Archives new Zealand/Te Rua Mahara o te Kawanatanga (Wellington Office); a cartoon (Archives Reference: AAAC 898 NCWA Q473) (page 73)
- Macmillan; an extract from *The Third Reich: A New History* by Michael Burleigh (page 76)
- An extract on page 81 from *Farm life in Northeast Scotland 1840–1914: the poor man's country* by Ian Carter is reproduced by permission of John Donald, an imprint of Birlinn Ltd (www.birlinn.co.uk)

- Pearson; an extract from *Changing Lives, Scotland and Britain* by Sydney Wood (page 82)
- Hodder; 2 extracts from *All Quiet on the Home Front* by Richard van Emden (pages 83 and 84)